How Not to Get Married:

A no-nonsense guide to weddings... from a photographer who has seen it ALL

George Mahood

This edition published 2019 by George Mahood.

Cover photo adapted from an original by Shelley Panzarella.

LIKE George on Facebook
www.facebook.com/georgemahood

FOLLOW George on Twitter
www.twitter.com/georgemahood

FOLLOW George on Instagram
www.instagram.com/georgemahood

www.georgemahood.com

Also by George Mahood

Free Country:
A Penniless Adventure the Length of Britain

Not Tonight, Josephine:
A Road Trip Through Small-Town America

Travels with Rachel:
In Search of South America

Operation Ironman:
One Man's Four Month Journey from Hospital Bed to Ironman Triathlon

Every Day Is a Holiday

Life's a Beach

All available in ebook, paperback and audiobook formats

Author's Note

All of the stories in this book are true. Many of the names have been changed to protect the privacy of individuals. Certain events and details have been edited into a different sequence to help the narrative. The wedding of Jen and Matt is an amalgamation of several different weddings.

I photographed both male and female civil partnerships during my career, but same-sex weddings were not made legal in the UK until 2014 – the year I stopped photographing weddings. I am very much in favour of same-sex weddings, but for the purpose of simplicity in this book, I have referred to couples as brides and grooms.

I photographed marriage ceremonies of several different religions, but the vast majority of my bookings were either Christian church or UK civil marriages, so my knowledge and experience is focused on these weddings.

To those who chose me to photograph their big day.

ONE

I switch off the car's engine and check the time. I am an hour early. Perhaps I was overcautious about the potential hold-ups on my 15-minute journey this morning. I am parked up outside a bride's parents' house at 8.30 a.m. ready to photograph what will be my last ever wedding.

I pick up a copy of a bridal magazine that is lying in the footwell of the passenger seat. Jen, today's bride, sent it to me because her venue is featured in this month's issue. I'm not a regular reader of bridal magazines, but I've got an hour to kill so have a quick flick through. A sentence in bold on one of the first few pages catches my eye: *'Choosing the colour scheme for your wedding will be one of the most important decisions you ever make.'* I want to start banging my head against the steering wheel, but a lady walking her dog down the street towards me makes me resist. I smile at her instead. She smiles back, then realises I'm a lone man suspiciously parked on a side street in the early morning reading a bridal magazine, and quickens her step.

I read the sentence again. *'Choosing the colour scheme for your wedding will be one of the most important decisions you ever make.'* Seriously? Has the wedding industry really come to this? Choosing the colour scheme for your wedding will not be one of the most important decisions you ever make. It will not even be one of the most important decisions you make about your wedding. Yet the wedding industry has grown into this huge uncontrollable beast that refuses to be tamed, and brides and grooms totally buy into this warped reality.

I have witnessed this hysteria from the point of view of both a participant and an observer. Having helped plan and organise my own nuptials, and experienced first-hand the highs, the lows, the magic and the madness surrounding the modern wedding, I then embarked on a career as a wedding photographer over a period of 11 years. Towards the end of my career I was photographing 50 weddings a year. I photographed over 250 in total, and this book is the culmination of my experience. I hope to share with you what I learned about weddings and offer a behind-the-scenes look at the job of a wedding photographer, shedding some light onto what it is like to document the most important day in the lives of these couples.

If you are planning a wedding, or hope one day to get married, you might pick up some useful hints and tips from this book about your own special day. You will most likely learn what not to do. If you are already married or were previously married, you will hopefully relate to many of the stories, and be relieved you don't have to go through it all again. If you plan on never marrying, this book could help reinforce your decision.

Weddings are an industry built on the notion of tradition: the dress you wear, the vows you say, the rings you exchange, the cake you cut, the bouquet you toss. These are all ingredients of what we believe is a traditional wedding. The whole institution of marriage epitomises tradition, and we blindly follow these customs because that is what is expected of us, and that is – how we believe – marriage has always been. But when you delve a little deeper, you discover that every element of the modern wedding has a very different origin. Many of these traditions have extremely dubious beginnings, some of them have seemingly been manufactured out of nowhere relatively recently, and others are, quite frankly, a load of absolute bollocks, yet we still consider them traditional.

Weddings have evolved over time and many traditions have remained, some have been adapted or constructed, while others have been completely forgotten. Take the bedding ceremony, for example. In many cultures, a marriage can be annulled if it has not been consummated. In the middle-ages, to ensure that a marriage was legally binding, this consummation often took place during the bedding ceremony. The married couple would be led to their bed at some point during the wedding reception, presented with gifts of food and wine, and they would do the deed in front of many of their guests who would act as witnesses that their marriage was legal. Surprisingly, I was never asked to document a bedding ceremony at any of the weddings I photographed. Perhaps this tradition will one day make a comeback and bridal magazines will boast the headline: *'forget the colour scheme, choosing which sexual position you perform in front of your friends and family will be one of the most important decisions you ever make.'*

As I sit in my car, parked opposite the house, I watch a flurry of friends, family and deliveries come and go. I can feel the butterflies in my stomach – the pre-match nerves I feel intently before every wedding. There is a fair amount of pressure working as a wedding photographer. It's a fast-moving, often unpredictable day, and you must be in all the right places at all the right times to capture the action, while still making sure you are as unobtrusive as possible. I accept the nervousness that I feel as a sign of focus, that my mind is on the job in hand. I know that if I ever stopped caring, if I ever stopped feeling this nervous, then I wouldn't be worthy of documenting such an important day. Thankfully I have never got to this stage. If anything, I am more nervous about this – my final wedding – than all the others that have come before it.

Today's wedding is between Jen and Matt. Jen and Matt were guests at a wedding I photographed at the beginning of last year. They loved their friends' photos and booked me as soon as they set their wedding date.

Like my wife Rachel and me, Jen and Matt went to school together but didn't become a couple until a few years later. They have been engaged for just over a year and have shared a house for the last four. Jen grew up in the house I am now parked outside, in a quiet village in the Northamptonshire countryside. Their wedding ceremony will take place in the church at the other end of the village, and from there we will go to the reception at a purpose-built wedding venue nearby, set in a couple of converted barns.

The hour has somehow passed (that bridal magazine was surprisingly engrossing), so I grab my camera equipment and head up the garden path to the house. Jen's parents live in a beautiful old sandstone cottage on a quiet lane on the outskirts of the village.

I knock on the door and a lady I assume is Jen's mum answers.

'You must be George, the photographer,' she says, seeing me standing there with a large SLR camera hanging over each shoulder. I am also wearing a black polo shirt with *George Mahood Photography* embroidered on it, just in case it wasn't obvious enough.

'I am indeed. And you must be… Jen's sister?' I say.

'Oh, I like you already,' she says, giving me a hug. 'I'm Fiona, Jen's mum. But I guess you already knew that.'

Being on good terms with the mother of the bride always makes my day a hell of lot easier.

TWO

So how did I become a wedding photographer? Did I, like many in the business, have a lifelong fascination with weddings and all that they symbolise? Did I used to watch weddings in films and on television and constantly fantasise about my perfect wedding? Was I so obsessed with the notion of weddings that I wanted to devote my working life to being involved in as many of them as possible?

No. Abso-fucking-lutely not.

Did I occasionally dress up in my mum's old wedding dress and pretend to be a bride? Well, yes, but I'll come to that later. The truth is I fell into wedding photography partly by accident, but mostly through desperation.

I was asked to photograph my first wedding at the age of 24 by two of my best friends from university. We had all shared a house together and they later became a couple. They knew I was a keen photographer, as I spent every waking moment between eating, drinking, sleeping and the occasional lecture, in the university's darkroom. I joined the Photographic Society, paid my annual subscription, and never went to a single society meeting. But my membership allowed me access to the darkroom facilities. Digital photography was still very much in its infancy, and film photography was still the industry standard. I did take a module in digital photography in my final year of university and we used some futuristic, state-of-the-art digital cameras that boasted a mind-blowing ONE megapixel, but by that point my love for photography, in whatever format, was already secured.

So, my first wedding booking was made on the basis that I spent a lot of time in the darkroom, and not on any actual evidence of my photos being particularly good. Basically, I was a man with a camera. In fact, I was a step up from that, I was a man with two cameras. For the occasion of my first wedding, I borrowed a friend's camera for the day, too.

The wedding was a fun and informal do; a ceremony at a church, followed by a casual reception in the beer garden of the local pub. It was fairly nerve-wracking, but the wedding went well, and I didn't feel too much weight of expectation as I was doing it as a favour, rather than for payment, and my friends very much liked the finished photos, or at least put on a convincing performance of pretending to.

It wasn't until this vote of confidence – being trusted to photograph a wedding – that I considered the possibility of pursuing photography as a career. But not wedding photography. Definitely not wedding photography. Wedding photography is avoided like the plague by the majority of professional photographers.

I had been working for several years as a Data Information Officer for a stroke charity, a job which was every bit as boring as it sounds, and I had been planning my escape for a while. I purchased one of the first available entry-level digital SLR cameras, quit my job, went travelling with Rachel, and returned home confident that I was beginning my new career as a freelance photographer.

I began shadowing a couple of local photographers on a variety of jobs. They soon started to trust me and see that I was a capable photographer, so began to pass jobs my way when they were double-booked, keeping their clients happy and taking a cut of the fee. I picked up a few of my own jobs along the way too. It was mostly PR and editorial photography – mechanics at work fixing engines, corporate bosses deep in thought during brainstorming sessions, official openings of new housing developments. It wasn't particularly thrilling stuff, but I loved it. I enjoyed the excitement and the variety of the jobs, and the fact that I was creating images that would appear in magazines – albeit obscure trade publications such as *Steel Toecap Monthly* or *Refrigerated Truck Weekly*, that perhaps only a handful of people would ever see. Still, I was a professional photographer.

Then, as quickly as they had arrived, the steady stream of photography jobs inexplicably dried up, and I was left without any work.

So, a similarly out-of-work friend (sorry, I mean 'freelance' friend) and I embarked on a penniless Land's End to John O'Groats trip to fill the time. We returned home and I started to write a book about it (*Free Country: A Penniless Adventure the Length of Britain*), while attempting to build up my photography business at the same time. Jobs did occasionally come my way, but they were sporadic and often not very well paid. I was still reluctant to advertise myself as a wedding photographer, as weddings are the one area of the photography industry that divides photographers like no other.

I spoke to a photojournalist friend who worked during the wars in Iraq and Afghanistan. He had photographed just one wedding during his many decades in the business and concluded that warzones were a far safer and less hostile environment than weddings. He stated categorically that he would choose Kabul over a wedding reception every time. I knew several other experienced photographers who had worked on some incredibly high-profile and demanding projects – action sports, celebrity portraits, large corporate events – and they all steered well clear of weddings. And I knew other photographers who stuck to the type of photography where you don't have to even speak to anyone, let alone try to make anyone smile, or act with any sort of urgency or spontaneity. I'm talking landscape photographers, food photographers, architectural and interior photographers, all of which are considered far less stressful and demanding areas in which to try and forge a career.

But despite all the advice against it, I decided that photographing weddings couldn't be that hard, could it? The one wedding I had photographed up to this point had – apart from one issue with a ruined film, that I will come to later – gone quite well. I had almost, dare I say it, enjoyed the buzz. Having quit my job to become a full-time photographer, and with very few photography jobs to show for it, I was left with little choice but to advertise myself as wedding photographer too.

I had taken my camera with me when Rachel and I had been guests at various friends' weddings and I had shadowed a couple of other wedding photographers, so I had acquired enough photos to assemble a basic portfolio. I had some business cards printed and a box of five thousand postcards made which included my business logo, a few sample photos, and my contact details. Each day – usually very early in the morning before dawn – I hand-delivered these postcards through letterboxes all around the town of Northampton where we lived. I posted them through every building with a letterbox – shops, restaurants, office buildings and residential addresses. I was advertising myself as a photographer for weddings, portraits, PR, commercial and music – spreading myself ridiculously thinly across the industry. I expected my phone to be ringing off the hook, and my email inbox to be overflowing. My phone didn't ring, and I didn't receive any emails. But for several weeks I kept delivering those damn postcards each morning. I had thousands of the bastards. What else was I going to do with them?

I had a map of Northampton town stuck to the wall in our spare bedroom and each time a street was complete, I marked it with a yellow highlighter pen to show that it had been delivered to. It was satisfying seeing the town gradually coloured in. We had no money, so while my friends with their proper jobs were out painting the town red, I was highlighting it yellow. Over the following weeks, my box of postcards slowly diminished. But still the phone didn't ring.

Eventually I received an email from someone who had seen my postcard. It was an enquiry about a wedding later that year. I met the couple the following evening, showed them my portfolio of photos on my laptop, and they agreed to hire me. They signed a contract and I was officially a wedding photographer. A wedding photographer with only one booking, but a booking nonetheless.

Over the following weeks and months, I picked up a few more jobs; a couple of weddings for the following year, but mostly PR jobs for periodicals like *Flower Arranging Monthly* and *Key Cutter Quarterly*.

My first paid wedding later that year went surprisingly well. They were a lovely couple, it was a beautiful venue, and my preparation had paid off. I knew the order of the day, I knew who the important guests were, and everything went to plan. I received a couple more bookings from guests at that wedding, and my list of bookings slowly grew.

Because I needed the experience and, more importantly, because I desperately needed the money, I started working for an established wedding photography business in the county called Sugar Sweet Precious Memories. (This is not their real name. The real name is much worse). Sugar Sweet Precious Memories was at the cheaper end of the scale. And when I say cheaper, I mean cheapest. They advertised by far the cheapest wedding photography package in the county, which was why they had so many bookings. This meant they paid their photographers a disgracefully low wage. The weddings tended to be cheaper affairs too – often second marriages, or registry offices. The coverage they offered ranged from one hour to four hours, either incorporating a few minutes of the bridal preparations until the guests sat down to eat, or just an hour of formal photographs after the ceremony. I would never meet the couple before the day, and due to the short timescale involved, never had a chance to build up any rapport or relationship with them during their wedding either.

To put this into perspective, for all of my own weddings, I would meet each couple twice before their wedding (once before they booked me, and again for the pre-wedding meeting to go through all the timings and details of their day, with occasionally an additional engagement shoot included too), and my coverage of the big day would usually extend to at least ten hours. This rapport is not only important for the photographer to get to know the couple, but it is perhaps even more important for the couple to get to know the photographer. These pre-wedding meetings enable the couple to feel more at ease in the photographer's presence, which then translates itself dramatically in the photos.

There was no opportunity to be creative during my weddings with Sugar Sweet Precious Memories. I was given a specific shot list that I was not allowed to stray from. For the four-hour package, it included a total of exactly 108 shots. This was based on the business owner Clive's earlier experience of photographing weddings with film and restricting himself to three rolls of 36 exposure film per wedding. He refused to accept the limitless potential of digital – or perhaps he thought you still had to pay per shot – and insisted that I didn't exceed the 108 shot limit.

The 'setlist' consisted of the usual staged photos, with the various formal group shots after the ceremony and specific shots during the service. It also included a section called '*FUN*' which were the ones I used to dread the most. There was nothing in the least bit fun about these photos. Clive insisted that the couples loved these photos. In my opinion, Clive was talking bullshit. They hated them every bit as much as I did.

These 'fun' photos included wince-inducing shots such as the best man standing outside the church before the ceremony physically trying to restrain the groom from running away. Hahaha, comedy gold! And then there was the one with the best man looking anxiously at his watch with the groom standing next to him with a look of mock anguish on his face that his bride wasn't going to turn up to the wedding. Fucking brilliant! What a humorous masterpiece! If the bride knew what a dreadful photography package she had agreed to, she certainly wouldn't have bothered showing up to her wedding.

The 'fun' continued after the ceremony with the overly cheesy shot of the groom and father-of-the-bride both planting a kiss on each side of the bride's face. Puke. But my all-time least favourite, which Clive claimed always got a good laugh from everyone at the wedding (what Clive failed to realise was that everyone was laughing at him) was this. The photo involved the best man leaning forward to try and kiss the bride on the cheek, and then with a look of rage, the groom would have his fist clenched tightly as if he was about to throw a punch at the best man. I usually managed to get the rage and anger to look quite convincing, but I think this was perhaps directed at me. I would always have to apologise and try and distance myself from Sugar Sweet Precious Memories. I felt extremely sorry for these couples having to pose for such ludicrous photos, but I felt even more sorry for myself for being required to take them.

I photographed about 15 weddings for Sugar Sweet Precious Memories over 18 months as my own list of bookings grew, and ironically didn't manage to acquire a single precious memory. But it is a job I was very grateful for. As a learning experience, my work for Sugar Sweet Precious Memories was extremely valuable. It helped me gain confidence in managing people for the formal group photos. I also learned to be less trigger happy. With digital photography, there is a tendency to just fire the shutter at anything and everything. Sticking to the 108 photo limit forced me to be more disciplined with my shooting style. But more importantly, working for Sugar Sweet Precious Memories taught me how NOT to be a wedding photographer.

'Come on through to the kitchen,' says Fiona, Jen's mum. 'The girls are having a quick bite to eat and making a start on the hair and makeup.'

I follow Jen's mum through to the kitchen. It's a big open-plan room, with the kitchen to the right and a dining area to the left. The dining table has been pushed against the wall next to the large bright patio window, and Jen and her bridesmaids are sitting around the room.

'Hi George,' says Jen, spotting me in the mirror. She is perched on a stool by the window, her hair being uncurled from some rollers. Jen is in her mid-twenties and has a warm smile and contagious laugh. She works in HR, I think. Or maybe that was the bride from last week.

'Hi Jen. How are you feeling? Everything seems very calm here.'

'Yeah, we are all very well thanks. I didn't sleep much last night.'

'That's normal,' I say.

'So I've been told. But we've had a nice chilled out morning. These are my three bridesmaids – my sister Cassie, and my two best friends, Shell and Katie. You've met Mum, and Dad is doing something in the garage I think.'

'He's tying ribbon on the car,' says Jen's mum. 'Trying to make it look posh.'

'It's really nice to meet you all. I'm George, the photographer.'

'Hi George,' all three bridesmaids say in unison.

'And this is Charlotte,' says Jen. 'She's doing our hair and makeup.'

'Hi Charlotte,' I say. 'Good to see you again.' I have met Charlotte at several other weddings, but it's never a good idea to start reminiscing about past jobs in front of a bride on her wedding day, so Charlotte and I keep the chitchat to a minimum. Jen doesn't want to feel like the latest on a never-ending conveyer-belt of weddings.

'Do you need anything from me?' asks Jen.

'No, you just carry on as you are. I'll just get some photos of you all relaxing. Is your dress hanging up somewhere?'

'It's upstairs in the middle bedroom. Go on up whenever you like. I've left the jewellery out that I'll be wearing in case you want a photo of that too.'

'Perfect. Thank you.'

Jen and Matt were in Paris to celebrate Jen's birthday when Matt proposed. He got down on one knee in the shadow of the Eiffel Tower. She said yes, obviously, otherwise I wouldn't be here today.

In an industry that is so meticulously planned, with every little detail of the day decided in advance, I like the unpredictable and often surprise nature of marriage proposals.

My proposal to Rachel wasn't especially romantic or lavish. But it was certainly spur-of-the-moment. I proposed during a picnic at a favourite spot of ours during a holiday in Devon. It was November and it was a spontaneous decision on my part. On the long drive down to Devon from Northampton, it suddenly dawned on me. *What was I waiting for?* We had been officially together for three years – having been best friends for nearly five years before that – and lived together for two. We had never discussed marriage, but the fact that we had bought a house together and two cats suggested it was probably inevitable. I thought of the words of the great Billy Crystal in *When Harry Met Sally*, *'When you realise you want to spend the rest of your life with someone, you want the rest of your life to start as soon as possible.'*

So, while shopping in a local town, I left Rachel trying on some clothes and went to the one and only jewellers in the area. Seeing as we had never talked about marriage, we had therefore never talked about engagement rings. I knew absolutely nothing about rings, or any form of jewellery for that matter. I did have a vague recollection that Rachel had once mentioned that she didn't like big stones on rings. She later decided, after having her new ring for a few months, that she did in fact like big stones on rings after all. But by that point it was too late.

The idea of engagement rings could be considered a little Neanderthal. *'Me give woman ring. Me own woman.'* Men don't have any outward sign to show they are engaged and 'taken', so it certainly seems a little sexist. I thought about telling Rachel that I had decided to forgo the engagement ring on the grounds that it was demeaning to women and that I was doing my bit for feminism. But then I figured, when all was said and done, she would probably prefer a ring.

So, dressed in a pair of scruffy combat trousers and a hoodie, I pressed the gold doorbell outside the upmarket jewellers. The elderly male shop assistant eyed me suspiciously through the window, a look of fear and concern on his face. He reluctantly buzzed me in.

'Can I help you?' he said as I entered.

'Hi, yes, I'd like to buy an engagement ring please.'

His look of distrust intensified. I don't know whether he thought I was going to rob the place, or if he just assumed I was a massive timewaster, or perhaps thought it unlikely anyone would want to marry a scruff-bag like me. Whatever his feelings, he didn't seem to think there was even a sliver of possibility that I would be buying a ring today.

I wanted to walk out of the shop and buy my ring somewhere else. This pompous prick didn't deserve my money. But I had already walked the entire length of the high-street and this was definitely the only jewellers in town. And I wanted to ask Rachel to marry me today.

'What sort of engagement ring are you looking for?' he said, in one single tone that showed no hint of enthusiasm.

'I don't really know. What do you have?'

'These are all our engagements rings,' he said, lazily waving his hands over several rows of rings in the glass cabinet, with diamonds ranging in size from a ball-bearing to a large cabbage.

'She's not a big fan of stones that stick up,' I said.

'I presume you still want a diamond?'

'Do engagement rings usually have a diamond?'

'Almost all of the engagement rings we sell are diamond.'

'Oh, ok. Do you have diamond rings where the diamond doesn't stick out?'

'We sell baguette-cut diamond rings, where the diamonds are set into the ring itself. We have two in stock but could order more from a catalogue.'

'Thanks, but I need it today. Are those the two there?'

'Yes. What size finger is she?'

'Um... I don't know. Just sort of normal sized, I guess.'

'There is no such thing as a 'normal sized' finger,' he said. He even did the air quotes with his fingers. The twat.

'Well, you know, just sort of average sized then. I've never thought of her fingers as being particularly big or particularly small.'

'How tall is she?'

'She's quite tall, I suppose. Just a little bit smaller than me.'

'This one will be a bit on the small side then,' he said, pointing to the cheaper of the two. 'This other one, however, is a size S which might be a better fit.'

'I like it. I'll take it.'

He looked a bit taken aback.

'Are you sure, Sir? Do you not want her to come and try one on?'

'No, I'm sure it will be fine.'

'Ok, very good, Sir.'

I only became a Sir the moment he realised I was actually going to buy a ring.

I had heard the rule of thumb that you are supposed to spend the equivalent of two months' wages on an engagement ring. This is a ridiculous rule and should be ignored by everyone. Weddings are very expensive occasions, and it would be a very bad idea to overspend before you've even popped the question. If your partner is the sort of person who will be disappointed with you not spending two months' salary on an engagement ring, I suggest that maybe you should find another partner.

16

The ring I bought Rachel was probably not considered especially pricey for an engagement ring. For me, it was the most expensive thing I had ever bought, apart from our house. But I didn't buy it because of the price. I bought it because it was the only one to choose from.

If you think the rule of thumb about engagement ring budgets is outdated, wait until you hear about the origin of the phrase '*rule of thumb*'. This phrase has its etymology in an old law that allowed a man to beat his wife with a rod or stick, providing it was no wider than his thumb.

With the ring tucked secretly into my jeans pocket, I met up with Rachel and we bought some bread, cheese and crisps for our picnic lunch. On the way back, I made up an excuse that I needed to pop back to the shops to buy some apples, so I left Rachel at the car while I jogged back into town. I had another important job to do.

Asking the father of the bride for permission to marry his daughter is a tradition that has declined over the years. Some consider it outdated and patriarchal because the concept implies ownership of the daughter by the father. However, having a daughter marry is a huge thing for any parent, so making your intentions clear seems like a polite way of encouraging a smooth and harmonious relationship with your in-laws. I agree that asking just the father is a little chauvinistic, as the impact on the mother is going to be just as big – perhaps arguably more so. Asking both parents seems a fairer thing to do.

Thankfully, asking Rachel's dad's permission went as well as it could have done. He answered the phone after a couple of rings, and I hadn't had time to get nervous or worked up about what I was going to say as it had all happened so quickly. I just told him I was planning on asking Rachel to marry me, and did he have any objections? He seemed surprised that I had even asked him, but delighted that we would be getting married – providing she said yes.

'Of course I don't have any objection,' he said. 'That's wonderful news. Good luck!'

I hurried back to meet Rachel at the car, trying to hide the grin that was spreading across my face; a blend of excitement and nervousness.

'I thought you went to get apples?' said Rachel.

'Shit,' I muttered. 'Err… I decided we had enough food.'

We drove to a nearby beach and then walked to eat our picnic at a boathouse we had been coming to for years. It was a cold November day, but it was dry and not too breezy. I hadn't thought through the logistics of the actual proposal. If I had had time, I might have tried something cheesy like concealing the ring inside the baguette. But we were a long way from the nearest hospital, so it's probably a good job I didn't.

Public proposals are all very well, providing the person you are proposing to would enjoy a public display of affection. If I had proposed to Rachel live on TV, or in the centre-circle of a football stadium at half time, or in the middle of a crowded restaurant, or in any public place for that matter, I know she would have been mortified, made a run for it, and I would probably have never seen her again.

I was too nervous to eat my lunch. I began fidgeting around with my pockets to try and ease my worries. I was still unsure how I was going to pop the question. Then, in a moment of panic – or perhaps inspiration – I pulled the drawstrings of Rachel's coat tight, screwing up the hood around her face so she couldn't see. Looking back, I'm surprised she didn't scream. Thankfully, she laughed from deep within her coat. Then, holding the cords tight in one hand, I jumped from my bottom onto my knees and reached into my pocket to take out the ring box. I released my grip on the cords and allowed her to untangle the hood from her face. Once she emerged from her coat and brushed her hair out of her eyes, her gaze moved to my hand which was holding the open box with the ring inside.

'Will you marry me?' I asked.

Her reaction was not what I expected, or had indeed hoped. Instead of saying yes and throwing her arms around me, she started crying. Then, through the tears and a big heap of snot, she said, 'You don't mean it.' Actually, it was more like, 'Yoooou *[sniff]*… don't *[sniff]*… meeeean *[sniff]*… iiiit *[sniff]*.'

'What do you mean? Of course I mean it.'

'Yoooou dooon't meaaan it,' she sobbed again.

'I mean it more than anything. I love you.'

This time she did put her arms around me, giving me a snotty kiss, sobbing into my shoulder and wiping her nose on my hoodie.

'Is that a yes?' I said.

'Yes,' she sobbed.

The ring was a perfect fit.

Throughout most of history, marriage proposals were not an elaborate affair. In fact, they weren't even a thing at all. In most cases, marriages were pre-arranged ties between families, usually negotiated in advance with the parents. Money and land would often change hands as part of the deal, and if the bride and groom ended up enjoying each other's company even remotely over the following years, then that was a bonus.

The act of genuflection – bending at least one knee to the ground as a sign of respect – has been documented as far back as Alexander the Great in 328 BC, who borrowed the idea from the Persians. Ever since, it has become a recognised way of showing respect, servitude to a leader, worship to a king or queen, or to receive a blessing or knighthood. It wasn't until the 1800s that it became a regular part of a marriage proposal.

Although I do like hearing about romantic and soppy proposals, I don't think any one proposal is better than another. It doesn't matter who asks who, or where or when it takes place. When all is said and done, the manner of the proposal is really not that important. Saying yes – or indeed no – to a marriage proposal is the only thing that matters. I know plenty of friends who discussed their proposal with their partner long before it happened. I also know people who have been so disappointed with the way in which they were proposed to that they made their partner do it again in a more romantic fashion. If your partner's proposal to you is a bit shit, don't make a big deal about it. Providing you want to spend the rest of your life with the person who is asking you to marry them, your marriage is far more important than the actual proposal.

My proposal was certainly not the most romantic, but judging by Rachel's reaction, it was a complete surprise to her. We got engaged in late November and married the following July. Which leads me nicely onto the subject of engagements.

During my career, I saw all manner of lengths of couples' engagements, ranging from only a month (in England and Wales, 28 days' notice must be given before a marriage can take place), to several years.

The reason for most long engagements is due to money, to allow the couple a chance to save up for the wedding of their dreams. There are obviously other advantages too. A long engagement is a bit like a trial marriage; if the romance dries up and you start getting cold feet during your engagement, then perhaps marriage isn't the best idea for both of you.

Some couples might want to get engaged to show commitment to each other, but not be at the right stage in their lives – a new baby, demanding job, sick parent – to be able to get married. I get that. What I don't understand is when couples book a wedding up to two, sometimes three years in advance, simply to get a particular venue, band or caterer that is fully booked for the next few years.

No band, caterer or venue is worth delaying your wedding several years for. Just get married somewhere else. Hire a different band. Find another caterer. Pick an alternative date. There are plenty of wedding suppliers out there who will be available. Organising weddings can be very stressful. If you set a date too far in advance, your wedding anxieties and worries will be stretched out over this entire period. While couples with a short engagement will have to put up with this stress for a matter of weeks or months, you will have to deal with it for years. You will be so sick of your own wedding by the time the date comes around you will wish you had blown your wedding budget on a trip to Las Vegas and been married by an overweight Elvis impersonator instead.

I was once exhibiting at a wedding fair and a young couple came over to chat to me and look through my sample albums.

'We've just paid our deposit for this venue,' they said. 'We can't wait to get married here.'

'It's a fantastic venue. You won't be disappointed,' I said.

We chatted some more about the package that I offered and the style of my photography. They were a lovely couple and seemed excited about my photos. I could tell from their enthusiasm that theirs would be a fun wedding to photograph. They started talking about the band they were going to book, and little details about their wedding day such as the favours and the background music that they were going to have played during the wedding breakfast.

'We would really like to book you to photograph our wedding,' they said.

'Fantastic. What date are you getting married?' I asked, hoping I was free.

'June 17th,' they said.

I glanced at my diary. This wedding fair was taking place in January 2013.

'A Monday? Cool. Yes, I'm definitely free.'

'No... sorry, we should have said. It's not actually this year.'

'Ok, next year? Is that a Tuesday? I'm sure I'm free.'

'Actually no, it's Saturday 17th June... 2017.'

'2017? Oh, wow. That's four and a half years away. I'm surprised the venue let you book it that far in advance.'

'I know. They didn't want to. It took a lot of persuading. We are just trying to get the crucial things sorted early, to give us time to plan all the other little bits of the day.'

'*Crucial things?*' I thought to myself. '*Like the background music and the bloody favours? My god, you two are in for a fucking long and boring 4.5 years.*'

'Oh... wow... that's great,' is what I actually said.

'So, are we able to book you? We are very happy to pay a deposit.'

I politely declined. I regularly took bookings for a year in advance. Sometimes 18 months. But four and a half years was far too far in the future to commit to. It's a good job I didn't take that booking as I photographed my last wedding at the end of 2014.

I would highly advise against very long engagements. So much could happen before your wedding day eventually comes around. Relatives or friends could die. Suppliers could go out of

22

business. The venue could close down. But more importantly, you will be so sick of thinking about your wedding, you will long for it all to be over, as will all your friends and family whom you will have bored the shit out of for so long. And once it is over, you will not know what to do with yourselves having had the thing looming over you for the last 4.5 years. It is really not worth it. If you are ready to get married now, but can't afford that special venue you have your heart set on, just go for a simpler wedding instead. Start spending the rest of your life with that special someone as soon as possible.

THREE

As Jen and her bridesmaids sit around sipping prosecco and having their hair and makeup done, they start reminiscing about the hen do in Benidorm.

'Remember, girls,' says Jen's mum, putting her finger to her lips. 'What happens on tour, stays on tour.'

'Your secret's safe with us, Mum,' says Jen.

The rest of the girls giggle, and Jen's mum's cheeks turn a deep shade of red. I'm intrigued to know more but know it would be unprofessional to pry.

As with other aspects of the wedding industry, the hen party – or bachelorette party, as it is known in the U.S. – has evolved at an alarming rate.

Female gatherings before a wedding can be traced all the way back to ancient Greece. The 'proaulia' was the recognised first stage of the marriage festival, where the bride would spend her final days before her wedding with her close female friends and relatives. Offerings were made to the gods to symbolise the bride's transition from childhood to adulthood. There would be laughter, gossip, eating and drinking, so in many ways the same as a modern-day hen do. The bride-to-be would then be required to watch a greased up pretend police officer strip naked and gyrate in front of her, before downing a cocktail through a penis-shaped straw. Ok, perhaps that last bit didn't happen in ancient Greece.

The term 'hen party' to refer to a gathering of females has been used in the U.S. since the 1800s, but it wasn't until *The Times* used it specifically in relation to a pre-wedding gathering in

1976 that the term became synonymous with weddings. Thanks largely to the sexual revolution of the 60s and 70s, hen parties became more and more adventurous as they developed into the huge industry they are today.

'Don't worry, those Benidorm photos will stay strictly confidential,' says Cassie, Jen's sister.

'They had better,' laughs Jen's mum.

'Better what?' says Dave, Jen's dad, striding into the kitchen while rolling up an armful of ribbon.

'Nothing for you to worry about, Dad,' says Jen.

'Hi, I'm George. You must be Dave,' I say, trying to divert the conversation away from the hen do.

'I am indeed. Nice to meet you, George. How do you cope with being in a room full of girls like this? I've been hiding in the garage for the last half hour pretending to be busy.'

'It's never boring,' I say.

'I bet you could write a book about the things you've seen and heard.'

Dave doesn't know I'm an author, but an idea springs into my mind.

'Ha, maybe I will one day!'

A combination of factors led me to decide to hang up my camera bag for good. My wife, three children and I, relocated from Northampton in the midlands, to South Devon in August 2013. Due to the nature of wedding bookings, I had dozens of contracted weddings until October 2014. Almost all of these were in Northampton – 250 miles away from where we now lived – but I had no intention of letting any of my couples down. So, I travelled back to Northampton at least every other weekend to photograph these weddings.

My intention had been to rebuild my photography business down in Devon, but things had not panned out that way. Living in such a rural area, there were far fewer weddings than there were in the bustling metropolis of Northampton. Nobody has ever described Northampton as a bustling metropolis, but it certainly is compared to where we live now. The wedding photography industry had also changed considerably in the decade since I started. Equipment was cheaper than it had ever been, and the internet, and social media in particular, was now playing a huge role in the success or failure of businesses. There were ten times more wedding photographers than when I started, and even though they didn't have the experience I had, they had better social media skills, more followers, more likes, more reviews and more enthusiasm. I wasn't bitter about these 'young guns'. I think they provided a welcome boost to the industry – more competition, more exposure, and more incentive to ensure customer satisfaction.

But these are all just excuses. In truth, I made very little effort to promote myself as a photographer in Devon. And when I say very little, I actually mean zero. I eventually published my first book, then wrote another and both were doing quite well. I didn't have the enthusiasm to try and start from scratch again as a wedding photographer, as the passion I once had for photography was now being channelled towards writing.

Before having children, and while my children were young, working almost every Saturday wasn't a problem. They were not yet school age, so weekends were no different to the rest of the week. I got to spend lots of time with the children during the week, and then would often be out all day working at the weekend. Once they started school, my weekends became more precious, and I was reluctant for my work time to be focused mostly on the days when the children were off school.

It's a long day photographing a wedding. I would be on my feet for about 12 hours, carrying two big cameras at all times, and often a heavy bag of lenses too. I used to enjoy the physical exertion of it, and that feeling of reward at the end of a hard day's work when I could sit back on the sofa and enjoy a beer. But recently, I had started suffering with back pain, which had got progressively worse through my final year as a wedding photographer. I put it down to carrying heavy camera equipment all day, coupled with the extended amount of time I was now spending sitting in a car driving to and from Northampton. It wasn't until a few months later that I was told I had a tumour slowing growing in my spinal cord. Don't worry, I survived (you can read all about that story in my book *Operation Ironman: One Man's Four Month Journey from Hospital Bed to Ironman Triathlon*). My decision to finish photography to focus on writing had already been made, but I was almost glad of the back pain as it reinforced the fact that I was making the correct decision to stop. I was not in any physical state to carry on as a wedding photographer. Perversely, my spinal cord tumour could not have come at a better time.

There was initial panic from brides and grooms when they heard I was moving to Devon. I think I would probably feel the same if my wedding photographer announced he was relocating 250 miles away a few months before my wedding.

Despite my reassurance that I would still be their photographer, couples would then panic that I would get stuck on the M5 and be late for the wedding, or perhaps not get there at all. This too was a valid concern, and it was something that probably worried me far more than it did them. So, to allay their fears, but more importantly my own, I always drove back to Northampton the day before a wedding and, depending on who was around, stayed the night with my parents, my in-laws or with a friend.

Despite spending the night in Northampton and usually being only a short drive from the wedding venue, I was still always paranoid about my car breaking down on the way to the wedding or getting stuck in traffic. This was so much of a concern for me that I would often arrive at the venue or the bride's house at least an hour early, as I had done this morning for Jen and Matt's wedding. I would then sit in the car, hidden away on a side street, until making my appearance at the exact time we had agreed.

'Wow, you are punctual,' the bride would say, not realising I had been parked around the corner since dawn.

I never did miss a wedding. Out of 250 weddings, I don't think I was even a minute late.

With Jen's dad Dave now out of the room again – presumably back hiding in the garage – the conversation turns once again to the hen do. I take this as my cue to leave the kitchen and go and photograph Jen's dress. On my way upstairs, I notice one of Jen and Matt's wedding invitations proudly displayed on a shelf in the hallway. It's a pale blue and white invitation, stylish and classic, without being over the top. Compared to some wedding invitations, this one is elegant in its simplicity. I have seen some ridiculously elaborate invitations. And by elaborate, I mean stupid.

I have seen invitations that arrived in their own personalised box wrapped in a ribbon. Why the hell would you send a card in a box? You can't get more efficient than an envelope. I've seen invitations sent in the form of a scroll, rolled up and secured with a wax seal. Again, senseless. I've seen wedding invitations that have been engraved onto thin slices of wood. Huh? I've seen wedding invitations sent with a personalised box of chocolates.

Very nice for the recipient, but unnecessary and a complete waste of money. If they can't come to the wedding, are they still allowed to eat the chocolates, or do they have to send them back? None of these elaborate (stupid) invitations are going to make your guests like you any more than they already do or make them any more likely to come to your wedding.

I understand the logic. You are planning one of the most important days of your life and you want to announce it in a special way. We fell into the same trap with our wedding invitations. When I say we, I mean Rachel. I would have happily sent my friends a text message containing the details of our wedding and *'reply Y or N'*.

Rachel spent weeks making our wedding invitations. Each one had a hand painted stained-glass mosaic thingy stuck to the front. I offered to help, but she didn't think I took enough care and attention when painting my first one, so I was demoted to the role of Chief Envelope Licker. We made countless trips to Hobbycraft to buy different shades of gold card, more bottles of glass paint, and different 'feels' of envelope. I tried to politely point out that it was a massive waste of her time and that the quality of our envelopes would not have any bearing on the response from our guests. Whenever I broached the subject – usually at about 11 p.m. when Rachel would be cursing and threatening to throw out one of the mosaics because she had used the wrong shade of red paint for one of the squares – I was shot down with an evil glare.

'But, LOOK AT IT!' she would yell. 'I can't send it like that, CAN I?'

'Why not? It looks lovely.'

'Because THIS square is supposed to be burgundy not sapphire, and THAT square is supposed to be crimson, not maroon.'

'I think it looks absolutely fine. I don't think anyone will notice.'

'Of course they will notice!' she shouted.

'I honestly don't think they will. And if they do, then I don't think they will... er... care.' I regretted my choice of words the moment they left my lips.

'What are you saying?'

'Um...' I said, not wanting to risk separation before we had even tied the knot. 'Send that one to one of my friends.'

'I'm not sending it to anyone. It's going in the bin.'

'Ok.'

Having got married, had children, and worked in a demanding career as a teacher, I think Rachel looks back and wonders how she ever had the time or inclination to hand paint all those invitations. We've received similarly meticulous cards from friends and relatives since, and Rachel has stared in bewilderment at the effort that went in to making them.

If you want to hand-make wedding invitations, putting a personal stamp onto your wedding, then that is absolutely fine. Some people will love them and appreciate your attention to detail. But the fact is, most people would be just as happy if you sent them the wedding details scribbled onto the back of a pizza takeaway menu, as if you had engraved it onto a gold trinket. It won't make any difference whatsoever to your actual wedding. A beautiful invitation does not a good wedding make, as Yoda probably once said.

Having said all that, it is possible to be creative with the wedding invitations without wasting a huge amount of your precious time, and provide your guests with something useful. We have received a fridge magnet wedding invitation, which we used to attach one of our kid's drawings to the fridge. We also received a wedding invitation printed onto a tea-towel, which gets regular use in our house. I was so fond of my tea towel I took it with me to France when I was taking part in an Ironman triathlon. I planned to use it to dry myself after the swim, but due to a mix-up with the bags, the tea towel disappeared, never to be seen again. After hearing of my plight, my friend sent me a replacement tea towel, with a note attached saying *'please don't dry your bollocks with this one.'*

Incidentally, during the making of our invitations, Rachel used to regularly get asked for ID buying glue in Hobbycraft (other dealers for glue-sniffers are available). I'm not sure Hobbycraft's Finest Premium Craft Glue is a favourite amongst glue-sniffers, but the regularity in which Rachel frequented the store definitely caused her to feature on some kind of watch list. I think they must have had a mug shot of her pinned up in the staff room.

I was just jealous. I haven't been asked for ID since my 18th birthday, and that was only because I basically begged the bouncer at Ritzy in Northampton to ask me for ID because it was the first time in my life I actually had a genuine ID, despite being a regular at Ritzy for several years with a slightly less genuine ID. Rachel also got asked for ID buying false eyelashes in Sainsbury's in her mid-twenties. As far as I am aware, there isn't a minimum legal age to buy false eyelashes, but it is because the product comes with a tube of glue. This tube of glue is so small that I doubt it would provide a fix for a glue-sniffing ant, let alone a fully grown human. Still, I'm just resentful because when I buy false eyelashes, nobody even bats an eyelid.

I take a couple of photos of Jen and Matt's wedding invitation – which will feature on a montage page in their wedding album along with the other details of the day – and make my way up to the spare bedroom where Jen's dress is hanging on the curtain rail.

The dress is beautiful. It is long and ivory-coloured and not too bouffy. That's about all I can say about it. Despite seeing hundreds of wedding dresses, my knowledge is a little limited.

The curtains are closed. This bedroom overlooks the garden, so I take a quick peek out to make sure there is nobody outside. I then open the curtains and spend a minute or so arranging the train neatly on the floor. It's a nice big window and the dress looks fantastic when backlit. I take some photos of the back and then carefully turn it around and get a few shots of the front, and some close-ups of the embroidery. I then turn the dress back to how it was and close the curtains. I always feel very nervous around wedding dresses, especially when I'm required to touch them, and I never underestimate the importance of the dress to the bride.

It's difficult to imagine a time when wedding dresses weren't white. But until the mid-19th century, brides from wealthy families would dress in vibrant, vivid colours, proudly displaying their wealth with heavy fabrics, furs, embroidery and jewels. Brides from poorer backgrounds would wear the nicest dress they owned or were able to borrow.

There are some historical documented instances of brides wearing white dresses – Philippa of England in 1406 and Mary Queen of Scots in 1559 – but it wasn't until the marriage of Queen Victoria to Prince Albert in 1840 that the white dress became the popular choice for weddings.

For many brides, choosing their wedding dress will be one of the biggest decisions of the day (perhaps second only to the colour scheme). I know of brides who have bought their wedding dress before being engaged. I even knew one bride who bought her wedding dress before she even had a boyfriend. I don't expect any potential brides out there to take advice from a cynical male former wedding photographer – what would I know about wedding dresses? – but I'm going to dispense my advice anyway.

The fact is this. Nobody at your wedding will care about your dress anywhere near as much as you. This is completely understandable. It is, after all, your dress and your wedding. How you look and feel on your wedding day is obviously a big deal, so I appreciate that choosing a wedding dress is therefore important to you.

Bridal magazines will tell you how particular styles are so 'in' this year, and how a certain designer or fit is the 'must have' type of wedding dress at the current time. It is all nonsense. It is only people who work for bridal magazines or are themselves wedding dress designers who will think a particular style is in or out of fashion. Most of the guests at your wedding will not have been to another wedding all year, possibly all decade. Nobody knows enough about current wedding dress trends to think, '*look what she is wearing, that dress is sooo last year.*' The truth is, all wedding dresses are ridiculous in principle. That's why they are only worn at weddings. They are completely impractical and over the top and not fit for purpose for any other day than your wedding. Embrace it. View your wedding as a fancy-dress party, where you are the only person who got the memo. Whatever you wear on your wedding day, you will look amazing.

Choosing a wedding dress is a very personal and important part of the wedding process for most brides, so I'm not going to criticise the ritual. But I have photographed over 250 weddings and I still can't tell the difference between an expensive wedding dress and a cheap second hand one, and I expect there are very few people who can. Price has very little effect on how good you will look in a dress. Buying a more expensive dress will not necessarily make you look better. I have seen brides wearing what I thought was something they must have been wearing for a bet, or through obligation to their mother, only to later discover it was a custom-made dress from one of the most expensive and sought-after designers in the country.

Conversely, I have seen the most beautifully dressed brides, and naively assumed they were wearing some pricey boutique dress, only to hear them confess that they had bought it from a charity shop, or off the peg in Primark. Wear a dress that suits you and makes you feel comfortable. Don't be fooled by the price tag. When choosing a dress, take an honest friend with you. Don't take your nicest friend. Honesty is more important than nicety. Your nice friend will tell you that you look stunning wearing a bin liner. Your honest friend will tell you that you look like you are wearing a bin liner.

More importantly, get a dress that fits. So many times, I have photographed brides who have obviously lost a lot of weight since their final fitting and spend their entire day trying to stop themselves slipping out of their dresses, or bought a size too small, anticipating that they would have lost weight before the big day, only to spend their wedding feeling and looking like a burst sausage.

Almost all wedding dresses are impractical, but don't get a dress that's so impractical you are unable to enjoy yourself. Remember that you will be wearing it for several hours. You'll be walking, standing, sitting, eating, dancing, drinking and most likely needing to go to the toilet several times during the day. If you do insist on a dress with a stupidly long train – that's fine – but don't then moan about it for the rest of the day when it gets in the way.

Once you have got through your wedding ceremony and finished the formal group photos, the fun begins. Now is the time to accept that your dress will not look so pristine at the end of the day. It is inevitable that at some point your dress will become stained with grass, mud, wine, or perhaps blood and vomit, depending on how lively your wedding is. Accept this. A dirty wedding dress shows that you have had a good day. You won't ever be wearing it again, so don't be overly protective of it. There is nothing more off-putting than a bride who spends her wedding warding off any potential signs of contamination.

What should you do with your dress after the wedding? You can't possibly sell it, can you? Why not? I would. Sell it and recoup some of that money you spent on it and know that your dress will get a life beyond you. But then I've never owned a wedding dress, so can't relate to how sentimental you might feel about it. If you insist on keeping it, don't be precious about it. It is just a dress. My mum's wedding dress ended up in our dressing up box and became the most popular item in there for my sister and me when we were growing up. Yes, I confess I wore it regularly. No, I don't have any photos, thankfully.

Rachel had her dress professionally cleaned after our wedding and then vacuum sealed into a bag at great expense. This bag was placed into a specially bought chest. This chest then became the stand on which our television stood, and the chest has not been opened and the dress not been looked at in 14 years. I keep joking to Rachel that I sold her dress on eBay years ago to buy the television that now sits on top of it. And in truth, I really should have. What good is it doing sitting in a chest that we can't even get access to?

'But what if Layla or Kitty want to wear it for their wedding?' argues Rachel.

'They won't,' I say.

'They might. It's a lovely dress.'

'It is. But did you want to wear your mum's wedding dress for your wedding?'

'No, but…'

'Exactly.'

The other option, which has increased in popularity, is a 'trash the dress' photoshoot. This takes my advice of not keeping a dress for posterity to a whole new level. At some point after the wedding, the bride wears her dress again, but this time wears it for activities completely inappropriate for wearing a wedding dress: climbing trees, swimming, rolling in mud, or paintballing. There is usually a photographer present to capture this 'trash the dress' moment.

I think it's a great idea, and I'm disappointed I was never asked to photograph one of these sessions. Yes, the dress is often damaged beyond repair, but at least you got some more wear out of it, and a different set of photos and memories than your wedding day. You can always stick it in the dressing up box afterwards.

Boxed up below Jen's dress I find her shoes. They are Jimmy Choos, which apparently means they are really nice. Or just really expensive. They look alright to me. Just like any wedding shoes, to be honest. They are ivory coloured with little studded crystals on the straps and a stupidly high heel.

Shoes are arguably more important than the wedding dress. Much of your wedding day will be spent standing and later dancing, yet still countless brides see their wedding day as an opportunity to buy that fancy pair of high-heeled shoes they have always dreamed of.

Right on cue, I hear Jen call up the stairs, 'Make sure you get a photo of my Jimmy Choos.'

'I'm already on it,' I say. But what I really want to say is, *'you are going to hate these fucking shoes so much later today.'*

And they always do. A bride will walk around her bedroom in them for a couple of minutes and decide they are the most comfortable thing ever, and that the quick lap of the room has 'worn them in' sufficiently. Then, unsurprisingly, later that day they are cursing their decision not to go for something more practical. You know that pair of sparkly, expensive, gold, high-heeled shoes you have always dreamed about owning? I agree that there is unlikely to ever be a better time to wear them than to your own wedding. But there will also never be a worse time. Your wedding is the one day of your life where you really don't want to be worrying about your feet. Those shoes will rub, they will cause blisters, your feet will hurt, you'll be begging to take them off. And, more importantly, your wedding dress is so bloody long nobody will even see your fucking shoes anyway. So, for everyone's sake, please wear something comfortable.

It's all my fault, though. Well, not just mine, but the whole male species. The popularity of high heels can be blamed on men.

High heels date back to the 15th century when Persian soldiers wore boots with a raised heel to help grip their horses' stirrups. This later caught on in Europe and heels served not just a practical use, but became fashionable, too. Aristocrats associated height with status and gaining those additional few inches reinforced their place in society.

It was not until the 16th century, when Italian noblewoman Catherine de Medici became the Queen of France, that women finally adopted heels. Catherine was a little under 5-foot-tall, so wore a pair of heels to her wedding, and women have had to suffer ever since.

But brides don't have to suffer on their wedding day.

Thankfully, many brides do seem to be stepping away from the idea of impractical shoes. Rachel wore flip flops when we got married. Partly for her own comfort, and partly because she didn't want to be towering above me during the ceremony.

I have photographed brides who have worn flip flops all day, brides who have worn their sparkly new shoes for the ceremony and then changed into flip flops later in the day, brides who have worn their favourite trainers for the duration – some secretly concealing them under their dress, and others proudly flaunting them. I have had a bride who wore wellies for most of the day – she somehow pulled it off – and I have had a bride who got married barefoot. Yet still, most brides choose to suffer.

'Oh, and there's a sixpence stuck inside one of the shoes,' shouts Jen. 'It belonged to my grandma. Could you get a photo of that too please?'

'Will do,' I call back.

As if wearing a pair of new high heels for a whole day isn't painful enough, many brides then crank up the pain to eleven by sticking a coin inside one of their shoes.

The sixpence in your shoe superstition is taken from the often-forgotten final line of the rhyme *'Something Old, Something New'*. The full ditty is *'Something old, something new, something borrowed, something blue. And a silver sixpence in your shoe.'*

The rhyme dates back to Victorian times, and the five different elements – all supposed to be incorporated into the bride's outfit – are supposed to bring her good luck in different ways.

Wearing 'something old' – perhaps handed down through generations – is supposed to protect any future children the couple might have together. How? I'm not sure. Perhaps a bride wearing an old item of clothing from her grandma will ensure that the bride and groom never actually have sex, meaning there will be no future children to need protection. Nowadays, the 'something old' has come to symbolise the idea of continuity, with a particular heirloom – perhaps a veil, ring or brooch – being passed down from generation to generation.

'Something new' is all about the future. Marriage is a new beginning, and the 'new' here symbolises the start of this new life together.

'Something borrowed' is supposed to symbolise happiness and good luck. By borrowing something from a happily married friend or relative, some of their happiness is being passed on to you. Traditionally, this was by the loan of some undergarments, but unsurprisingly this tradition died out. I can't think of a worse way to begin married life than finding out your new wife is wearing a pair of your mother-in-law's knickers.

'Something blue' is meant to symbolise fidelity. Although surely agreeing to get married should be considered evidence enough?

'Do you, Mark, take Daisy to be your lawfully wedded wife?'

'Well, to be honest, I love her, but I am not sure I can trust her to be faithful to me.'

'But I'm wearing a blue ribbon in my hair,' says Daisy.

'In that case…. I do!' says Mark.

And finally, the 'sixpence in the shoe' symbolises prosperity. It was traditionally given to the bride by her father and this superstition does have some merit. In every single case where this tradition has been followed, this simple symbolic act has caused the bride to become more prosperous. She is richer every time, by the sum of six pence.

I understand that it's a nice little rhyme, and it does enable the bride to put a bit of thought into what she wears on her wedding day. But it is, essentially, a load of bollocks. I have seen plenty of brides stressing out on the morning of their wedding because they have lost their sixpence, or they forgot to borrow Auntie Catherine's brooch, and now the marriage is doomed before she has even taken her vows. The truth is, nobody knows exactly when this tradition started, or who wrote the little ditty. It is believed to have started in the Victorian era, but it is unclear for what purpose. I have no doubt that when it was created it was done so for a little bit of fun, not something that would be rigorously followed and stressed about nearly 200 years later.

Imagine if whoever wrote it had been feeling a little different on that particular day and gone for a slightly more creative rhyme.

'Something alive, something dead, something slimy, something red, and a flowerpot on her head'.

It would have made my job so much more entertaining.

There are a few other accessories laid out on the side – a brooch, garter, necklace and some fancy-looking hair clips – and I lay each one out in turn on the rustic wooden dresser and capture some close-up photos for the album.

Another more recent trend is to have words or initials on the soles of the bride's shoes, so that when she kneels at the altar, they will be visible to the congregation. Popular examples include the bride's initials on the sole of one shoe, and the groom's on the other. Another common one is to have *'I'* and *'DO'* on each of the bride's shoes – usually created with diamante stickers under the arch of the shoe – and sometimes *'me'* and *'too'* on the groom's. It's a little tacky, but also quite cute and harmless. I have also photographed a few weddings where the groom has knelt at the altar, with the words *'HELP ME'* on the soles of his shoes, clearly visible for all to see except the bride and the vicar.

Jen has opted to graffiti her expensive Jimmy Choos with these *'I DO'* diamantes, and it gives me another photo opportunity as I carefully balance her precious shoes against a dresser and photograph the soles. Fortunately, Jen has not made the same mistake as one of the brides I photographed (at least, I think it was a mistake). When sticking on her diamante words, she got her left and her right mixed up, so the soles of her shoes read 'DO I'.

FOUR

I make my way back downstairs and join Jen and her bridesmaids in the kitchen-diner. Jen is in the final stages of having her makeup done. She seems both excited and nervous, as do all her bridesmaids.

Bridesmaids are such an important and pivotal part of modern weddings that it seems difficult to imagine weddings without them. Their role, amongst other things, is to show support and solidarity to the bride on her special day. But the role of the bridesmaid hasn't always been about companionship. Bridesmaids once had a far more important duty. They weren't there simply to hold the bride's train, pose next to her for photos, or help her take a pee. They were tasked with the responsibility of guarding the bride's life. In ancient times, the job of the bridesmaid was to keep the bride safe from either kidnappers or evil spirits, almost forming a human shield around her. Traditionally, they would dress the same as the bride and all wear veils to disguise their identity and cause confusion to any potential villains. Bride kidnapping happened throughout history in all corners of the world. Terrifyingly, it still occurs in some parts of the world today.

Jen has three bridesmaids, which is an ideal number. There is an inclination in recent years to have an army of bridesmaids, almost as though it's a popularity contest. *Look how many best friends I've got. Aren't I popular?* Don't do it. Just choose a small handful of your closest friends or family. Don't assume that So-and-so will be offended if you don't pick her. Because if you pick So-and-so then you'll only upset What's-her-name, and then you'll have to ask What's-her-name too, which in turn will annoy Thingamabob, so Thingamabob is suddenly a bridesmaid too, which angers Whatsherface, and before you know it, you have 18 bridesmaids.

When you have an excessive number of bridesmaids, your day will feel claustrophobic and chaotic. During the morning's bridal preparations – which should be a time of excitement and anticipation shared with your closest friends and family – you will be surrounded by women arguing over hairspray, taking too long in the bathroom and competing for your attention. Also, the more bridesmaids you have, the more attention is taken away from you. For some brides who feel anxious about being the centre of attention, maybe that's intentional, but it's honestly not worth the hassle.

If you have a friend that does get offended about not being given the role of bridesmaid, then they probably aren't a very good friend, and certainly would not be a very good bridesmaid. A good friend, and therefore a good bridesmaid, will honour and respect your decision whoever you choose.

Once you have decided on your bridesmaids, please let them have a say in the dress they will wear for your wedding. Far too often, I have seen bridesmaids spend the entire wedding day making bitchy comments to each other behind the bride's back about their horrible dresses, and how the colour makes their skin look bad, and the fit makes them look fat, suggesting that the bride has chosen such revolting dresses to deliberately make herself look better than the bridesmaids. In some instances, it is entirely possible that she has. But, for the sake of everyone, let them be involved in the choosing – even if you ultimately have the final say. It will make them much happier, and they too can feel special and enjoy the day, without feeling the desire to slag you off behind your back.

Charlotte, the hair and makeup artist, has done an excellent job. She has had a bride, three bridesmaids and a mother to attend to, and has single-handedly done the hair and makeup for all five, without looking in the least bit flustered or rushed. I am always impressed by the composure and patience involved with doing hair and makeup. One bride I photographed was a professional hair and makeup artist, and not only did she do her own hair and makeup on the morning of her wedding, but she did her mother and five bridesmaids too. She seemed to enjoy the challenge and said it helped distract her from getting too anxious about the wedding.

You listened politely to me giving my opinion on wedding dresses, but what the hell would I know about hair and makeup? I know very little (nothing) about the actual processes or the techniques and styles involved, but I feel like I do know enough about the finished results to be able to at least pass comment.

I understand that brides and grooms want to look their best on their wedding day. It goes without saying. But what I simply don't understand, is why you would want to look so different you become unrecognisable.

I have seen far too many naturally beautiful brides sit down in the makeup chair and by the time they are done they look like a member of a bad KISS tribute band. I've seen spray tans so severe that instead of looking radiant, they end up looking radioactive. I've seen hairdos so extravagant it was a genuine concern whether the bride would fit in the car. I've seen many grooms double-take when they've looked down the aisle, clearly thinking *who the hell is that?* and not in a good way.

And it's not just the women. The same can be said for men. I've seen plenty of spray tans gone horribly wrong, eyebrow plucking taken way too far, and experimental haircuts the day before a wedding. Your partner is marrying you because of how you look every day, not how you look when you're dressed up for Halloween. Less is more. Don't overdo it.

The church in which Jen and Matt are marrying is at the other end of the village. It's only a five-minute drive, but I am getting anxious that I should head on down there to get some photos of Matt and his groomsmen before all the other guests arrive. Jen is planning on getting into her dress early, so I decide to stick around for a few more minutes. That sounds a little voyeuristic of me. I should clarify, I always leave the bride and bridesmaids to get into their dresses without me snapping away. I then ask them to give me a shout when the bride is in her dress and just in the final stages of being laced or buttoned up.

I get the call from Jen's mum, so head upstairs and tell them all how amazing they look – on this occasion I don't need to pretend (at some weddings, I do), because they are all glowing (not in a radioactive way). I take some photos of Jen's mum and the bridesmaids helping to lace up Jen's dress, and thankfully they all seem to be well practiced and make light work of the task. I have been at weddings where bridesmaids have been frantically typing '*how to tie a wedding dress*' into YouTube with minutes to go before the ceremony. I even had one wedding where all attempts to lace the dress failed, and so the dressmaker – who fortunately lived nearby – was summoned to the wedding to save the day.

There will be time to get photos of Jen and her bridesmaids when they arrive at the church. There is no point posing for photos in a cramped bedroom, so I say goodbye and then jump in my car and drive the half-mile to the church.

The location of your ceremony is likely to be one of the first decisions you make when organising your wedding. Church weddings are nowhere near as popular as they once were. The number of regular church goers has fallen to a record low and this has been mirrored by a consistent decline in religious weddings over the last few decades. Just 27% of UK weddings now take place in a religious building.

The failure to embrace same-sex marriages, controversy within the organisation, and an unwillingness to modernise have all been partly to blame, but this shift away from religious venues is not all down to the failure of the church. It is largely due to a dramatic increase in the number of licensed wedding venues available. It used to be a straight choice between a church or the local registry office. Nowadays, most venues that cater for weddings are also licensed to conduct marriage ceremonies on the premises too. And many of these are stunningly beautiful locations: converted barns, botanical gardens, golf courses, stately homes, orangeries, or even the pitch of your favourite football team.

It used to be claimed that civil ceremonies – in dark, soulless registry offices – were a lot less romantic than a church wedding. This is far from true nowadays. Often civil ceremonies can feel even more romantic, with smaller, more intimate buildings. They are usually a lot warmer than a big old church too. Most civil ceremonies still have readings, there are still vows, exchanging of rings, and personal touches can be added to make the occasion unique.

Churches and weddings, however, have such an entwined history that it's difficult to envisage a time in the future that they are shunned completely. Rachel and I got married in a church. I am an atheist, but I respect and understand the importance of religion. Rachel is not particularly religious but liked the idea of a church wedding, and so did her family, and although I did feel a little hypocritical, I was happy to go along with it. Regardless of your religious beliefs, it's difficult to argue against the fact that most places of worship are damn fine buildings.

Our vicar told us how one day he had driven up to his church one Saturday afternoon, and there was an entire bridal party of about 20 people all gathered outside the church gates. He went into panic mode and burst from his car.

'I'm so sorry,' he said. 'Am I supposed to be officiating your wedding ceremony today? I had nothing in my diary.'

'No, no, you're alright,' said the bride. 'We just got married at the registry office downtown, but we thought we would come out here for some photos 'cos the church is so pretty. Is that ok?'

After the relief swept over the vicar that he hadn't missed a wedding, he then momentarily felt a little aggrieved that they were taking advantage of his church. This soon passed when he realised that despite their decision to have a civil ceremony, they were also acknowledging how beautiful his church was. And for that he was honoured.

'Of course,' he said. 'Take as long as you like.'

Getting married abroad is becoming more and more popular too. There are obviously many advantages: you can pick a more unique and picturesque venue than you might find closer to home, the chances of good weather are better – although still not guaranteed – and you can combine the wedding with your honeymoon, which can be very cost effective.

Despite the inconvenience of the distance, weddings abroad can often be less stressful to organise, as you are forced to hand over a lot of the duties and responsibilities to the venue. This can be seen as a negative for some people too. Do you trust them to implement your plans? Can you rely on suppliers if you haven't had at least one face-to-face meeting?

Getting married abroad may also mean that many of your guests won't be able to make it. Some couples consider this a good thing, and sure, it does help whittle down your guest list to those that are dedicated enough to make the journey. But what if you have an elderly relative who you would love to be at your wedding, but they are not well enough to travel? Or one of your best friends is struggling financially and won't be able to afford to come? These are all considerations that you need to factor in if planning to marry abroad. Getting married abroad is considered by some to be a little selfish. But it's your wedding, so be selfish.

I park a little down the street from the church. I made the mistake at my first few weddings of securing a space right next to the church. The first problem with this was it was difficult to photograph the bride's arrival at the church, or the bride and groom leaving, without my ugly beaten-up Toyota Avensis photobombing the shot. I also, inevitably, got blocked in by other cars and so couldn't leave to get to the reception until most of the wedding guests had left first. The benefit of experience has taught me to park a little way away to ensure a smooth and easy getaway.

It is October but warm for the time of year. I am dressed in a pair of black trousers and a black polo shirt. I went through a series of jackets and jumpers during my photography career but used to get so hot photographing weddings that I would remove my jacket or jumper and then accidentally leave them at venues scattered around the country.

I like weddings at this time of year. Autumn and winter weddings, in my experience, attract a different kind of bride and groom. They are often more relaxed, lower-maintenance, and have reassuringly realistic expectations of their day. Jen and Matt are no exception.

Picking a date is one of the first priorities of a bride and groom. It is not as important as the colour scheme, obviously, because that is one of most important decisions you will ever make in your life, but it is definitely up there. Historically, in the UK at least, the summer months are usually the most popular for weddings. August, closely followed by July, are the top two preferred months for couples to marry.

According to the Office of National Statistics website (it's basically Pornhub for data nerds), August was the most popular month for weddings back in 1947 – the earliest year they have data available.

During the 1950s and 60s, there was a huge spike in weddings for March in the UK, making it the most popular month by far for both these two decades. Perhaps this was because of a desire to make the most of the beautiful spring flowers? Or perhaps to embrace the change in weather after a long cold winter? Actually, no. The reason that March was the most popular month during these two decades was because of tax. Specifically, the tax allowance for married men. During the 50s and 60s, a married man got an additional £120 (the equivalent of over £2000 in today's money), compared to a single man. But a loophole meant that this allowance was paid regardless of how long the man had been married. So, many weddings were squeezed in during March, before the end of the financial year, in order to receive a backdated payment for the previous year.

The government put a stop to this at the end of 1968 (it only took them two decades to realise what was going on) by changing the calculation to take into account how long a couple had been married. By 1970, the trend of March weddings had ended, and the popularity had swayed back in favour of the summer months once again.

The reason for August's popularity is obvious. It's the warmest month, long hot days, glorious sunshine, flowers in bloom, vibrant green grass and dry underfoot. Except this is only in an ideal world. The weather is notoriously unpredictable in the UK, especially during the summer, and it is not uncommon for it to rain for days at a time during July and August.

So, while August and July are still the most popular months, there has been a definite sway in recent years towards off-season weddings. Autumn and winter weddings are on the increase. If you get married in the winter, your expectations for the weather are set pretty low. You assume that it will be shit, so you can only be pleasantly surprised by good weather. If you have paid premium prices for an August wedding, hoping for bright sunshine, there is a chance your wishes might come true, but there is also a strong chance of disappointment.

Every part of a wedding is planned down to the most microscopic detail. It's ironic then, that the weather – which can make or break a wedding, if depended on too heavily – is the one thing completely out of your control.

Despite being out of their control, that doesn't stop couples obsessively checking the weather forecast on an hourly basis in the build up to the wedding. At almost every pre-wedding meeting I ever had with brides and grooms, there would be some mention of the weather. The British are famously obsessed with talking about the weather, but if you combine it with an obsession about weddings, it gets a bit out of hand.

'I've checked the 30-day-forecast, and it looks like there might be a bit of rain between 10 and 11 a.m. but then it should be dry for the rest of the day,' a bride would say to me at our meeting a month before her wedding.

'Ok, that's great. Although, I don't think you can rely too heavily on a 30-day-forecast. It will most likely change.'

'What? Do you think it's going to rain in the afternoon too?'

'Er… no… I hope not. It might not rain at all.'

'Oh, I hope so. Hang on, I'll check again to see if it's changed yet. Nope, it still says rain between 10 a.m. and 11 a.m.'

Seeing as the issue of the weather came up with almost every single couple I met, I had a well-rehearsed spiel that I gave whenever concerns were raised. It was based on my experience of photographing weddings on some of the hottest, coldest, wettest, windiest and cloudiest days I had ever known. My words of wisdom were this, and I meant them sincerely.

'Whatever type of weather you have on your wedding day, there will be a positive outcome. If it is a sunny day, you will be blessed with bright blue sky, lots of time outside, and happy smiling guests. Everyone is happy when the sun shines. Sunny days are great for everyone… except the wedding photographer. Photographers won't complain about the sun, as getting good weather at a wedding is always welcomed, but bright sunshine means strong shadows and changes in contrast. It means people squinting. Throw a white dress into the mix, and you make the job a whole heap tougher. If it is cloudy or overcast on the day of your wedding, you will get better photos. Clouds are a photographer's best friend. The light is flattened, there are no shadows, no glare or squinting, and a photographer can snap away in perfect conditions, in any direction they choose. So, if you wake up to an overcast sky on the morning of your wedding day, you might be disappointed, but I will be fist-pumping.'

I didn't always say the fist-pumping bit.

'What about rain?' the bride would interrupt. 'Good luck finding a positive spin for rain.'

'Ah, well,' I would begin, 'rain is incredible at creating a fun atmosphere at a wedding.'

The bride and groom would look at me with confusion.

'How so?'

'You see, if it's a beautiful day and the sun is shining, your guests will be spread far and wide across the venue. Some will be enjoying drinks on the lawn, others will have taken a wander around the grounds, and some will prefer to be sheltering from the sun and heat indoors. When it is raining, everyone is in the same place, and when you have all your friends and family in one place then you have the most enjoyable party atmosphere. Some of the most fun weddings I have ever photographed have been when it chucked it down all day.'

The bride and groom would slowly nod in acknowledgement, showing that I had reassured them.

'And…' I would continue, 'it is very unlikely that it will rain ALL day. So even if it is wet on your wedding day, the chances are we will be able to nip outside at some point to take some photos.'

This is also true. It would often mean delaying the group shots until later in the day, or even occasionally sneaking out with the bride and groom during the meal. Out of all the weddings I photographed, I only ever had to do all of the formal group shots and couple shots inside on one occasion. One in 250 is pretty good odds that you will have at least some of your photos taken outside.

St Peter's – the church in which Jen and Matt are marrying – is a beautiful old sandstone church, built in the 13th century. The workmanship of these old churches is phenomenal, and even as an atheist, I can't help but be grateful for organised religion for giving us such incredible buildings.

There is no sign of Matt or his groomsmen outside the church, so I make my way down the gravel footpath to the door. Two large autumnal floral arrangements sit either side of the entrance.

The familiar smell greets me as I make my way inside; slightly damp and musty but, combined with the earthy scent of the stone and the sweet aromas of the flowers and the candles, making a pleasing combination. I will miss this smell. They should bottle it and sell it as perfume. Eau de God. It won't be the last time I step in a church, but unless I have a sudden change of beliefs, my visits will become far less regular after today.

Reverend David is laying out hymn books on the pews. He looks up and smiles as I walk over to say hello. He has two other churches in his parish, and I have photographed four or five weddings in which he has officiated. He's a tall, skinny man, with brown hair and thick-rimmed glasses. He looks to be in his early 50s and seems quite youthful for a member of the clergy.

I met my fair share of vicars during my decade of wedding photography. If you have read any of my other books, you might think that I have a bit of a vendetta against the church. In my book *Free Country*, we are denied a place to stay by a vicar on the Scottish borders, and in *Every Day Is a Holiday*, I even go as far as writing a letter of complaint to an archdeacon about a vicar who was rude to me at a wedding. These are both unique cases. I don't make a habit of complaining about vicars. For the most part, I got on very well with all of those officiating the weddings that I photographed. Occasionally I would meet a registrar or vicar who, although well-meaning, was almost comically bad at their job. I've seen officiants conduct ceremonies who have been so inarticulate it was hard to distinguish if they were reading marriage vows or practising Mandarin.

I always made a point of introducing myself to whoever was conducting the ceremony before the wedding, and to ask them what their policy was regarding photography during the service. The responses would differ from venue to venue and could range from not being allowed to take any photos in the building whatsoever, to being allowed to snap away throughout the ceremony. Some would insist I stayed at the very back of the room and others would allow me to stand almost wherever I liked. I didn't want to be too visible during the service so always tried to tuck myself away somewhere discreetly and used a long lens and no flash to be as unobtrusive as possible.

There are some 'creative' photographers out there who have ruined the reputation of respectful wedding photographers. And by creative, I mean twattish. I've been a guest at a wedding where the photographer was lying down on his stomach in the aisle for the duration of the ceremony. It was like he thought his covert position made him invisible. Little did he realise that the entire congregation was watching him, rather than the bride and groom. I was intrigued to know what his photos looked like from such a bizarre and unflattering angle. I saw another photographer who felt she was so friendly and intimate with the bride that she snapped away throughout the ceremony – with a large flash – at a distance seemingly closer to the bride than the groom was. I kept having to remind myself who was getting married to who.

Whatever rules and restrictions the officiant implemented about photography, I accepted them. It wasn't worth protesting or trying to push the limits. And to be honest, if I was told I couldn't take any photos during the ceremony, it made my job a whole lot easier.

Reverend David is very relaxed about photography and trusts that I will not interfere. I doubt he knows my name – even though it is written on my shirt – but I know he recognises my face.

'Hi Reverend David,' I say, stretching out a hand to him. 'Good to see you again. I'm George, Jen and Matt's photographer. I've photographed a few weddings you've conducted.'

He shakes me firmly by the hand.

'Yes, good to see you. Have you seen Jen yet this morning?'

'I've just come from her parents' house. She seemed very relaxed. She was already in her dress by the time I left 15 minutes ago.'

'Crikey, she's keen. The service isn't for another 45 minutes.'

'Does your usual policy apply regarding photos? No flash, no excessive clicking, but you're happy for me to stand over in the corner towards the front?'

'Yes absolutely. You know what you're doing.'

'Great, thanks. Have you seen Matt yet? I thought he would be here by now.'

'He popped in about 20 minutes ago. They tied all the flowers to the pew ends and then he said they had to go and sort something out down the road. I think he meant they were going to the pub, but he probably didn't want to tell me that.'

'Ha, I see. I'll wander down there now. Thanks. I'll see you in a bit.'

Right up there with the splendour of old churches are old pubs. There is something magical about stepping into a pub, stooping your head to avoid the low beam, and ordering a pint in an establishment that has been serving beer to customers for hundreds of years. The menus have changed, the décor has been updated, and the prices have certainly inflated (I'm starting to sound like my dad), but the essence of the public house is the same as it always has been. The Red Lion, about 100 metres from St Peter's, is no exception.

But, unfortunately, I'm not here to buy a pint. I'm here to work.

During the rare opportunities that I was a guest at a wedding, I had a sensation of complete liberation. I was able to relax into the day, feeling very much in tune with how the wedding was going to unfold, but without the pressure of having to document it.

I also tended to take advantage of being able to have a few drinks. Rachel and I were once guests at the wedding of a friend of hers. It had been a particularly busy year for me with weddings, but this was the first in over a year where I was a guest. Despite only knowing three people at the wedding, including Rachel, I was very excited about the prospect of being off-duty. We were seated at a table with all the other mateless guests and I got chatting to a guy called Tom – a PE teacher from Manchester – who was very attentive at keeping my wine glass filled, and I was very happy to go along with it.

Late into the evening reception when the disco had been in full swing for an hour and I was feeling a little worse for wear, the DJ cut the music and made an announcement.

"Ladies and Gentlemen, we now have an exciting little interlude for you all. Two guests will be battling it out on this dancefloor in a dance off."

We all whooped. Who could it be? Were the bride and groom going to have a dance off with each other?

"First up, please welcome contestant number one... Tom."

"Isn't he the bloke from our table?" said Rachel.

"Yeah, he's a nice guy," I slurred. "He's a PE teacher. I bet he's quite athletic. Although, I think he's very drunk. My money is still on him, though."

Tom walked onto the dancefloor, clapping his hands high above his head. He was well up for this.

"And, please welcome onto the dancefloor, Tom's challenger… George."

We all whooped again.

"That's you," said Rachel. "You're George."

"I know I'm George, but I'm not THE George. I haven't challenged Tom to a dance off. There must be another George."

"Err…" said Rachel. "No, it looks like it's definitely you."

I looked up and Tom was in the middle of the dancefloor pointing directly at me. I looked behind, hoping to see another George eagerly accepting Tom's offer but there was nobody there. He beckoned for me to join him. I shook my head adamantly and made it clear I had no intention of having a dance off with him. He then threw an imaginary lasso around me and started trying to haul me onto the dancefloor. I cut his imaginary rope with my imaginary scissors and he fell dramatically backwards onto the floor. The crowd all laughed. Tom was loving this. He threw another imaginary lasso at me. I stepped out of the way of it, folded my arms and shook my head.

"Go on!" said Rachel. "He's challenged you. You have to accept."

"No way! Why would I want to have a dance off with him?"

Then the DJ took the microphone again.

"C'mon George. We are all waiting. The dancefloor is yours."

"No!" I said. "I'm not having a dance off! This was nothing to do with me."

Then the crowd – none of whom I knew – started chanting my name and so Rachel gave me a gentle shove from behind and

I was suddenly standing with Tom in the middle of the otherwise empty dancefloor.

The next few minutes are a bit of a blur. Partly because I was so drunk, but mostly because I have tried to block it from my memory.

I have a vague recollection the song that began playing was Michael Jackson's *Billie Jean*. There was no backing out now. The DJ announced the start of the competition and Tom began first. He opened with a modest warmup, gyrating his hips – Michael Jackson-style – and waving his arms in time with the music. He then signalled to me that it was my turn. I tried to copy him, and made an adequate effort, only not quite so in time with the music.

Tom then broke into an 80s robot which I tried my best to emulate. The crowd, sensing my incompetence, were encouraging and supportive at this point, and cheered along. Tom progressed through a series of different dance moves, including an impressive rendition of The Worm, as he rippled his way across the dancefloor on his chest. I couldn't compete with that. I shook his hand, acknowledging that he was the winner, but he refused to accept victory and motioned for me to continue. The crowd all chanted my name again so I attempted my own version of The Worm, which resulted in a mortifying new move I invented that I would like to trademark The Dead Slug.

Tom then began a series of spectacular breakdancing moves, each more complicated than the last. I kept trying to leave the dancefloor, but he refused to let me, and my attempts to copy him became more and more pathetic. The bastard had completely set me up. This was simply an excuse for Tom to show off his skills and humiliate me. How the hell had I ended up having a dance off with someone I had only known for a couple of hours, at a wedding where I only knew three people?

Just when I didn't think things could get any worse, Tom started walking around the dancefloor on his hands. I was struggling to walk around the dancefloor on my feet. I conceded defeat yet again, but still he wouldn't let me stop. Even the bride was cheering for me to give it ago. So, I tried. After a couple of unsuccessful attempts to even get both feet off the ground simultaneously, I took a run up and used the momentum to try and get up onto my hands. This time both feet momentarily left the ground, but my complete lack of upper body strength meant my drunken arms couldn't support my weight, even for a fraction of a second. They gave way beneath me and I crashed face-first into the sticky dancefloor. There were collective winces from all those around the room.

This was a new low. I was lying in the middle of an empty dancefloor at a wedding, with my face squashed against the floor. For a moment, I thought I was going to be required to attempt it again, but fortunately the DJ put me out of my misery and cut the music, declared Tom the winner, and invited everyone to fill the dancefloor once again.

Rachel helped me to my feet, struggling to breathe because of her laughter, and I staggered to a seat at the edge of the room.

"Wow, that was quite a spectacle," said Rachel, in-between giggles.

Tom walked over and shook my hand. I told him he was a dickhead and I hated him. He laughed and half-heartedly apologised.

Rachel reminded me the following morning how I had spent about 10 minutes in the queue for the buffet later that night, declaring to the mother-of-the-bride that although Tom was the deserved winner, I felt I was the People's Champion.

Thankfully, I never saw anyone from that wedding ever again.

Matt, his best man and his two ushers, are all standing at the bar of The Red Lion enjoying a quiet drink before the long day ahead.

'Hi George,' says Matt, shaking my hand. 'How are you?'

'I'm very well thanks,' I say. 'More importantly, how are you?'

'Er… yeah. Pretty nervous actually. This is my best man James and my two ushers – Rob, my brother, and my mate Nathan. Guys, this is George the photographer.'

'Hi,' they all say.

'Nice to meet you all,' I say, shaking them each by the hand. 'What did you get up to last night?'

'Just a couple of beers and then we played on the Xbox for a bit. Fairly early night in the end,' says best man James.

'Very sensible,' I say. It was surprising the number of weddings I photographed where the groom (and on a couple of occasions the bride) spent most of their wedding day trying to recover from the previous night's drinking. I even had one groom who wore sunglasses the entire day to hide his bloodshot eyes and removed them only briefly during the ceremony when the registrar insisted on it.

Matt seems different today. He was an outgoing, confident guy on the previous occasions we met. This change in character on the wedding day is not unusual, particularly for a groom. Men, in my experience, don't seem to be very good at thinking ahead. In the build-up to their wedding, the bride would, in most cases, have the more active role with the organising. She would often get nervous and stressed in the weeks and months leading up to the big day, while the groom would remain relaxed in comparison, always thinking that the event was something far off in the future and not something that should cause too much worry at the present time.

And then the wedding itself suddenly arrives, and in most cases, preparations have all gone to plan. The hard work is done, and the bride feels a huge sense of relief. There is nothing left for her to do other than enjoy her meticulously planned day. She is usually calm, relaxed and ready. The groom – not so much. There is a sudden realisation that today is the actual day, and he is hit by a wave of fear. Not through doubt – well, not very often – but just because of the sense and scale of the occasion, and what they are about to go through. It was evident at nearly every wedding I photographed. Fortunately, this fear and panic felt by the groom is only temporary. It passes quickly and has usually completely disappeared by the end of the ceremony.

After the vows have been said, I could visibly see the relief on the faces of the bride and groom – especially the groom – knowing that the scary part of the day is done, and now they can enjoy the party. It's a feeling I experienced myself at my own wedding.

'You'll be absolutely fine, Matt,' I say. 'It's perfectly normal to feel nervous. All grooms feel like this.'

'Do they?'

'Absolutely. I felt exactly the same as you when I got married.'

'That's good to know. Any tips? Will it last all day?'

'No, it'll soon pass. This will be the worst it gets. You'll feel more relaxed as the day goes on. After the ceremony, you won't even remember feeling any nerves.'

'I hope you're right,' he says, taking a swig of his pint. 'This beer seems to be helping a little.'

My role at a wedding was more than just a photographer. Especially during those crucial hours before the ceremony – when I would spend a lot of time with both the bride and groom before their whirlwind of a day began – I often felt like the reassuring voice of calm. All these experiences and apprehensions were new to them, but I had witnessed it all many times before, and I was often able to help solve many last-minute problems, answer any questions, and try to reassure them that everything was going to be alright.

In between taking photos, I was called on to perform many other tasks: cooking pizzas, retying bouquets that had come undone, pinning on button-holes, ironing shirts, changing a car tyre, ferrying guests to or from the church, feeding a hungry pet or opening bottles of champagne. I enjoyed these extra duties that I was trusted with. Perhaps I was being treated as a skivvy, but I viewed it as a compliment that I was able to offer more than just the click of my camera's shutter.

James and Matt have been best friends since primary school. James – along with the ushers, Rob and Nathan – is doing a fine job of helping to relax Matt and calm his nerves. As with bridesmaids, the role of the best man has changed dramatically over the years.

The origin of the best man can be traced back to a time when marriages weren't the mutual love story they largely are today. The bride would often be kidnapped against her will or against the will of her family. The groom would have a chosen ally to stand beside him to act as his private security guard. The best man wasn't chosen for being the groom's 'best' friend, he was chosen for being the best swordsman.

Ushers were just an additional level of security. Nowadays, ushers can be extremely valuable. They can provide help with handing out orders of service, directing guests to their seats, helping those who need assistance, rounding up groups for the photos, calling everyone through to eat, liaising with suppliers, handing out gifts during the speeches and just generally being useful. If your ushers aren't useful, there's very little point in having them. Then they are just blokes in matching suits who get in the way.

But, as with bridesmaids, don't feel the need to have loads of ushers just to keep your friends happy. If anything, having a big group of ushers only serves to alienate those friends that didn't make the cut. I had two best men at my wedding and no ushers. I have a nice big group of friends, and there was no obvious cut off I could make to include some and not others. And our wedding ran just fine without those additional blokes in matching suits.

My suggestion about allowing bridesmaids a say in what they wear to your wedding does not apply to the groomsmen. In my experience, I never once saw a best man or an usher complaining about the colour of his shirt or the cut of his suit. Blokes have the luxury of pretty much knowing exactly how they will look – a suit is a suit – and not caring too much if they look ridiculous for a day.

Matt and his friends went to Riga, Latvia's capital, for his stag do. When I last saw him at our pre-wedding meeting, he had only been home for 48 hours. He hadn't given too much away, but it sounded like they had an eventful few days. I went to Berlin for my stag do. A group of 22 of us made the trip. The location was picked mostly because we could get a flight and three nights in a cheap hostel for less than a weekend in Brighton.

I was the first of my friends to get married, and so got away lightly with regards to stag-do humiliation. I had to wear some bling jewellery, a pair of weird sunglasses and drink a few random cocktails, but that was about it. My friends knew that because none of them were married, whatever pranks they pulled on me now would come back and haunt them on their own stag dos.

I was later the best man for two of my friends and was much crueller than they were to me, as I knew I was safe having already married. Beware of married best men, they are always the worst.

I was given a lap dance on my stag do. From one of my male friends. He had gone to the effort to shave ALL over, he wore a wig, a bra with ample padding, lots of makeup and a pair of fishnet stockings. I was blindfolded and seated in the middle of the room in an Irish pub (when in Berlin...). He gave me a very impressive, and perhaps slightly sensual, lap dance for about five minutes before I wrestled him to the ground.

During the 'lad culture' era of the 1990s, stag parties got out of hand with grooms being regularly strapped naked to lampposts with cling film, flights being diverted due to drunken behaviour, and entire stag parties ending up behind bars in some obscure city in eastern Europe. The long-standing negative reputation of stag parties causing all sorts of trouble and havoc seems to have lessened in recent years, and it feels like we have passed peak stag do. Venues have cracked down on large groups of men, airlines have a zero-tolerance policy for bad behaviour, and men have perhaps become more self-conscious and aware of the reputation that stag parties have gained.

A few years ago, I phoned up the owner of a holiday property in the Peak District to try and book it for a group of 16 of us for a friend's stag do. I hadn't dared mention the S word, but when she came out and asked me directly, 'is it for a stag do?' I told her it was, but promised that we would be very well behaved. 'Oh, that's absolutely fine,' she said, 'I was just being nosey. I have never had any problems with stag parties. It's the hen parties that cause the trouble. They always leave wine stains on the sofas and carpet and they get makeup on EVERYTHING.'

As with the hen do, the stag do – or bachelor party as it is also known in the U.S. and Buck's Night in Australia – can be traced back as far as ancient Greece. In the 5th century BC, Spartans would eat, drink and toast to celebrate the night before a groom's wedding. They were also popular amongst the upper-classes in Tudor England, with Henry VIII reportedly being a big fan. In fact, he liked stag-dos so much he decided to get married six times. Imagine being a guest at one of Henry VIII's stag dos. I can't imagine there would have been any best man alive brave enough to force Henry VIII to wear a mankini.

FIVE

I let Matt and his crew enjoy their beers and I take a few casual photos of them chatting together at the bar. The ceremony is in 30 minutes and they will shortly be heading back to the church.

I ask James, the best man, if he has the rings.

'Yes, I do. I've only checked my pockets about 10,000 times already this morning.'

'Would it be ok for me to borrow them for a couple of minutes?'

'Err…'

Best men get very anxious when I ask them if I can borrow the rings.

'It's ok,' I say. 'I won't leave your sight. I'll just be over there in the corner getting a couple of photos of them.'

'Err, ok then. Please look after them and bring them straight back.'

'I will. I promise'

I carry the rings over to an empty table in the corner. The corner of an old pub might not seem like the most photogenic place to take photos of wedding rings, but you only need two things to get decent photos of the rings: good light and a good surface. A good surface can be anything from the top of a stone wall, to a shiny marble top kitchen work surface, to a wrinkled brown leaf, an order of service, or in the case of this pub, a gnarled wooden table.

I can sense James watching me from the bar as I carefully balance Jen's wedding ring on Matt's and take some closeup photos with my macro lens. I return the ring box to James, and as predicted, he opens the box to make sure that both rings are there and that I haven't lost one or substituted them for something cheaper.

'Just checking,' he says.

Thankfully, I have never lost a ring. Although, I did once come very close. As with today's wedding, I had borrowed the rings from a best man, but on this occasion I had placed them on an area of wooden decking in the back garden of the groom's house. As I stood up after taking the photos, the strap on my camera bag knocked the bride's ring from its perch and it slipped through a gap between the boards.

My heartrate raced and my forehead beaded up as a sense of panic overcame me. The best man appeared at the back door, presumably after hearing my volley of expletives.

'Everything ok?' he asked.

'Yes. Absolutely fine! Thanks. I just stubbed my toe. Nearly done here. I'll be inside in a minute.'

He continued to loiter in the doorway. I needed to distract him before he noticed I was only taking photos of one ring.

'Could I possibly have a glass of water?' I asked.

'Yeah sure. There are soft drinks set out in the kitchen. Help yourself. There's food there too if you want.'

'Oh, thanks,' I said, but still he lingered. 'Um… could you go and ask Dave if he would like a photo of his cufflinks?'

'Ok?' he said, with a look as if to say, '*why the hell would Dave want a photo of his cufflinks?*'

He disappeared inside and I scrambled onto all fours at the edge of the decking. There was a small gap and I was able to squeeze my arm and shoulder underneath and stretch for the ring which was fortuitously nestled on some moss within reach. I emerged from beneath the decking just as the best man reappeared at the door.

'Dave says no thanks about the cufflinks.'

'Ok, no problem,' I said, dusting off the bride's ring and putting it back in the box with the other. 'Here you are. I'm done with these. Make sure you don't lose them!'

I have also had a best man accuse me of not giving him the rings back after photographing them, which led to me getting into a frantic panic thinking I had lost them somewhere, only for the best man to realise he'd put them in a different pocket of his jacket.

It is very rare for a ring to go missing. It does happen though, and friends of mine discovered during the exchange of rings that one of theirs had somehow disappeared between the church gate and the altar. A replacement ring was borrowed from a random uncle so that the rings could be exchanged during the ceremony, and the actual ring was later found by the wedding photographer – not me – in the gravel outside the church.

Even as far back as the ancient Egyptians, 6000 years ago, evidence exists of rings made from hemp and reeds being exchanged between partners. Circles have had a close symbolism with eternity for thousands of years, as they represent the never-ending cycle of life and love. It is thought that the practice of wearing a ring on the fourth finger of the left hand also dates back to these ancient Egyptians. They believed that this finger contained a special vein that ran directly to the heart (it doesn't – it's the same as all your other fingers) and it later became known as the *vena amoris* – the vein of love.

When Rachel and I were planning our wedding, I decided that I wouldn't have a wedding ring. My dad has never worn one, and I don't wear any other jewellery or even a watch, so the idea of a ring felt a little weird. Rachel initially seemed to agree.

'I don't think you should wear a ring,' she said. 'It wouldn't suit you.'

'No, I don't want to wear a ring,' I said.

'WHAT? Why don't you want to wear a wedding ring?'

'I… but… you…'

'Do you not want people to know you are married?'

'You know that's not the reason. You just said you didn't think I should wear a wedding ring.'

'Well, I didn't realise you were so against wearing one.'

'I am not against wearing one. I am very happy to wear one if you want me to.'

'It's not that I want you to wear one, it's that I want you to want to wear one, even if you don't actually wear one.'

My look of confusion didn't do much to ease the situation.

The following day we went ring shopping together. I tried on a couple of different rings and Rachel finally conceded, 'No, rings look really stupid on you. You shouldn't wear one.'

'But what if I want to wear one?'

'Do you?'

'I'm happy to want to wear one if you want me to want to wear one.'

It turns out she didn't want me to want to wear one that much, so I didn't bother.

Two years after we were married, I decided I did in fact want to wear one after all. By this point, I don't think Rachel even wanted me to want to wear one. I'm not sure what changed in me, but I suddenly felt the desire to wear a wedding ring. So, we went out and bought one.

It took me a long while to get used to wearing a ring, and in those first few months I fiddled with it constantly. Once, on an aeroplane, I was playing around with it so much that it fell onto the floor and then disappeared under the seat in front of me. I spent the next ten minutes on my hands and knees, crawling down the aisle apologising to people as I searched under their seats. I eventually found it between the feet of an elderly lady three rows down.

On another occasion, I was in the pub watching England lose a crucial European Championships qualifying football match. It was a tense and frustrating game and when it was looking like England would be defeated, I was fiddling with my ring, but my slightly swollen hands prevented the ring from sliding the full length of my finger. In my frustration, I tried to force it, and it slipped over my knuckle and then flew off my finger, into the air, and a long way across the crowded pub. The room was packed full of football fans, all standing squashed together. We had arrived early and got seats at tall bar stools around a table on a raised area, so my ring sailed a good 10ft over the crowd's heads and into the mosh pit.

'Oh fuck!' I shouted.

'What?' said one of my friends.

'I've just fired my wedding ring across the room into the crowd.'

'You did what?'

I explained what had happened and instead of offering to come help look for it, my friends sat there and laughed at me. It helped lighten the mood of England's dismal performance but didn't help my predicament that I was a married man who would be returning from a night at the pub without his wedding ring. I tried briefly to look for it, but it was almost impossible to even walk through the crowd, let alone search for it on the floor.

The final whistle sounded ten minutes later. The advantage of a dreadful match is that the supporting fans don't like to hang around long after the final whistle. There was a lot of booing, shouting and swearing, and the pub emptied fairly quickly.

My friends and I spent the next 20 minutes crawling around the pub floor looking for my wedding ring. We were joined by the landlord and a few bar staff, but I was eventually faced with the realisation of leaving the pub without it. I decided to wake Rachel when I got home and confess, expecting to receive a barrage of abuse. Instead she just laughed and said, 'you are such a dick,' and rolled over and went back to sleep.

My phone rang at 1.30 a.m. that night. It was the landlord of the pub. I had left my phone number with him in case it turned up. And it had. While vacuuming the floor at the end of the night, one of the members of staff had found it under a table leg and had rescued it before it disappeared inside the vacuum cleaner's dust bag forever. I was of course mightily relieved, and have taken better care of my wedding ring ever since.

Different types of wedding rings have come in and out of fashion over the centuries, taking various forms, but rings have remained an important part of the marriage ceremony. Gimmal rings were popular in the 16th and 17th century. These consisted of two interlocking rings and the bride and groom would wear one each from the time of their engagement to their wedding. During the ceremony, the rings were re-joined together, and the complete piece was worn by the wife.

Wedding rings are sometimes engraved with elaborate patterns or embedded with expensive stones, but nowadays the most popular wedding rings tend to be plain bands. Considering how elaborate and excessive almost every other aspect of the modern wedding has become, it is quite heartening that wedding rings have remained relatively simple.

All the attention is given to the engagement ring. A big expensive diamond engagement ring. But it hasn't always been that way. The first recorded use of a diamond engagement ring was in 1477, but they were somewhat of a rarity and confined mostly to the aristocracy. Engagement rings went out of favour during the 16th century, with the focus of importance turning back to the wedding ring.

After World War I and the Great Depression of the 1930s, the popularity of engagement rings declined considerably. This lasted for several years until arguably one of the most successful marketing campaigns the world has ever seen.

Struggling sales, and a fall in the desirability of diamonds, forced the De Beers group – the largest diamond company in the world at the time, with a monopoly over the entire industry – to hire a marketing agency to boost sales. A young copywriter named Mary Frances Geret came up with the slogan, '*a diamond is forever*' and the future of the diamond engagement ring was secured. This phrase has been used in every single De Beers diamond advert since 1948. It is estimated that 80% of today's proposals involve a diamond engagement ring. So, the 'traditional' diamond engagement ring is only so closely associated with weddings because of a hugely successful, and fairly recent, marketing campaign.

Advertising Age magazine awarded '*a diamond is forever*' the title of 'Slogan of the Century' in 1999, presumably pipping Birds Eye Potato Waffles' '*waffley versatile*' to the top spot.

SIX

'It's 12.40 p.m.,' says Matt. 'We should probably get to the church. Guests will start arriving soon.'

The dutiful groomsmen all down what's left of their pints and they head for the door.

I take some photographs of them walking through the village as we make our way back to the church. I spot a nice stone wall bordering the churchyard and we stop to take a few posed shots, before freeing them up for their other duties.

Although not a regular churchgoer, Matt knows Reverend David well from their pre-wedding meetings and from when he and Jen attended church to hear their banns being read.

The banns are a notification of a couple's intention to marry and a chance for the church congregation to pray for the couple, or put forward a reason why the marriage can't lawfully take place. It is a legal requirement in the Church of England for banns to be read out in church before a wedding can go ahead. These banns are not just read once. They are read three times, on three Sundays, and can be spread over a number of weeks. The couple are expected to be there when the banns are read out, to receive the prayers and blessings of the congregation, or hear any objections. They are read out in the home parish of both the bride and groom.

Rachel's parents lived in a neighbouring parish to where I grew up, so the banns were read at her own parish too. So that was a total of six Sundays in church before we were even married. I could hardly wait. It would be a small sacrifice for a lifetime of happiness.

My only slight issue was that the reading of the banns took place on a Sunday morning. Sunday morning was when I spent time with the other love of my life: Abington Stanley Football Club. Abington Stanley FC was a football team I helped set up in 2003, the year before Rachel and I got married. A group of school friends and I – by this point in our mid-twenties – wanted to start playing competitive football again, and we knew we were unlikely to all be able to sign for the same team, let alone get picked to play, so we decided to set up our own Sunday league team. We managed to scrape together a few more friends and then some friends of friends and we finally had 11 players, and Abington Stanley Football Club was born. Our club was named after the area of Abington in Northampton in which we lived, and Accrington Stanley – an English league club made famous by a TV advertisement for milk in the 1980s.

We were truly awful. For the first few seasons we finished either bottom or second from bottom of the league, ahead of Gunners or Real Roochers Reserves, who were the league's other whipping boys. We were at the bottom of Division Eight. There was no Division Nine, so we had nowhere left to be relegated to. It was ten weeks before we had our first win, and that was a cup game against a team with only eight players, and it didn't do anything to aid our lowly league position. But we loved it. I was club chairman, which meant absolutely nothing, and centre midfielder. What I lacked in skill, I made up for in dedication, and I would only miss a match if I was injured so severely I couldn't stand.

Rachel and I once woke up at 4.30 a.m. to drive back to Northampton from a holiday in Devon to get there in time for a 10.30 a.m. kick-off, after I had convinced Rachel that 'my team needed me'. Abington Stanley lost 9-0 that day, and I did momentarily question whether my dedication was worth it. Six weeks of banns readings, and six weeks of missed matches was going to be really hard for me to take.

I was all set to go to church on the Sunday morning of that first week, when I got a text from Abington Stanley's manager saying that one of the players had had to pull out. He asked if I was definitely unable to play as they didn't have any spare players, and, well, my team needed me. We always only had 11 players. It was very rare for us to ever have any substitutes. I showed the text to Rachel, laughing to try to convey the fact I had no desire to play.

'I suppose you can play this week. It sounds like your team needs you,' she said, while smiling and rolling her eyes at the same time.

'But what about the banns?'

'I can go on my own. We don't both have to be there.'

'Really? Are you sure you don't mind?'

'No, it's fine. There will be another five Sundays after this.'

I gulped.

'Thank you.'

The following week, Abington Stanley were short of players again. My team needed me. Again. Again, Rachel told me to go and play football while she went to church.

The third week, the same happened again. Who'd have thought?

'Rather than go through this charade every Sunday,' said Rachel. 'Why don't you play football and not bother coming to any of the reading of the banns?'

'It's not a charade. They are genuinely struggling for players.'

'I know, I know, your team needs you!'

'They do. But I don't have to play.'

'Well, what would you rather be doing, coming to church or playing football?'

'Ermm, coming to church?' I said, completely unconvincingly.

'It's fine. I honestly don't mind.'

So, while Rachel attended church for six weeks in the build up to our wedding, I played football – my church. I did feel very guilty about it, but I knew Rachel would be more annoyed with me if she felt I was resenting being at church when my team needed me.

Guests begin arriving for Jen and Matt's wedding. Matt still looks nervous, but he's smiling and putting on a brave face. I can sense he is starting to relax as more and more of his friends and family greet him. I soon work out who the key players are – the mother and father of the groom, grandparents and other close family – and I make sure to get plenty of photos of these important people. At 12.55 p.m. Matt is ushered inside by Reverend David as Jen's car will be leaving her parents' home shortly.

Brides and grooms are not supposed to see each other before the wedding ceremony. Why? Because it's bad luck, of course. Everyone knows that.

But why is it bad luck? How can seeing the person you want to spend the rest of your life with be the cause of bad luck? It can't. It's another silly tradition that has become ingrained in wedding culture.

This one dates back to the days when arranged marriages were common across the world. After all the hard work and planning involved in arranging a marriage, it was essential for the wedding to actually go ahead. The uniting of two families through this marriage was, in a sense, an important business transaction. It was feared that if the couple met before the wedding, one or the other might realise they had been paired up with some ugly minger and decide to do a runner, ruining the entire deal. To prevent this, couples were kept apart until the day of their wedding. Their marriage ceremony was often the very first time they laid eyes on each other.

I shouldn't write about arranged marriages as though they are an ancient tradition. Arranged marriages are still commonplace in many parts of the world. In fact, some studies suggest that over 50% of all marriages in the world today are arranged.

Back to the tradition of it being bad luck for the bride and groom to see each other before their wedding. When it comes to non-arranged marriages, there is no logical reason whatsoever why a bride and groom shouldn't see each other on the morning of their wedding. If they do see each other and one of them gets cold feet (or suddenly has the realisation that their fiancée is, in fact, a minger) and does a runner, then it's probably for the best, and will save them from becoming another divorce statistic later.

It actually makes a lot of sense for a bride and groom to see each other beforehand. It should help make them feel relaxed, waking in their own home, having breakfast together and perhaps even getting ready together. They then get a chance to compose themselves before seeing all their guests, and maybe even have some of the formal photographs taken before the ceremony. This seems to be an increasingly popular way of doing things, especially in American weddings.

But I must confess, I really like the illogical tradition of a bride and groom not seeing each other on the morning of the wedding. It helps give the wedding ceremony a bigger sense of occasion. I like the innocent secrecy of a bride choosing a dress that she then keeps hidden away from her partner until the day of the wedding, refusing to even divulge the tiniest clue about its appearance, so as not to risk bad luck. I also like the childish thrill of the logistics of making sure the bride and groom's paths don't cross on the morning of the wedding, all because of a ridiculously unreasoned superstition. And most of all, I love the look on a groom's face when he turns to see his soon-to-be-wife walking down the aisle in her dress. It gets me every time.

I can still remember my feelings, the sense of drama, nervousness (and nausea) all prevalent on the morning of my wedding, only to have it all replaced by an all-empowering sense of joy when I turned to see Rachel walking down the aisle. You miss out on this feeling if you've already posed for photographs together outside.

One venue I photographed at regularly had a big set of curtains over the window of the bridal suite where the bride got ready the morning of her wedding. This room was situated across a small courtyard to the barn in which the wedding ceremonies took place. It was possible to see through these curtains from inside the bridal suite, but impossible for anyone outside to see in.

The bride and her bridesmaids would be able to watch the guests arrive at the wedding, without fear of being spotted. This included being able to see the groom. Apparently, it is ok for the bride to see the groom, just not the other way around. All the brides I photographed at this venue thoroughly enjoyed having a secret look at the person they were about to marry, who was suited and booted and completely unaware that they were being watched by their fiancée from the other side of a curtain. It was very entertaining for me as a photographer as I was permitted to move through the curtain between the two camps.

On one occasion, a groom – who had arrived nice and early for his wedding and was completely oblivious to the fact his fiancée could see him – lit up a cigarette out in the courtyard.

'Oh my god! What the hell?' muttered the bride, staring through the curtain in disbelief. 'Danny told me he had quit! The sneaky git.'

The bridesmaids and I reassured her that it was probably just a one off to calm his nerves, and when I met up with Danny a few minutes later I warned him about the questioning he might receive later and to get his excuses prepared. I also slipped him a piece of chewing gum.

As well as the arrival of the groom, it was hilarious to watch the bride and bridesmaids provide a running commentary as the rest of the guests made their way into the ceremony room.

'Awww, doesn't Auntie Cathy look beautiful. I LOVE that dress. I wonder where she got it.'

'There's cousin Daryl. He's come over from Tenerife. I haven't seen him in about ten years. He hasn't changed a bit.'

'Oh, there's the lovely Megan looking beautiful as ever. And there's Martin, her wanker of a boyfriend. I so wish she would finish with him. She could do SO much better.'

'Oh my goodness, look how cute little Matthew looks in his suit. He's only two. Isn't he adorable? I just want to eat him up.'

It was such fun being a fly on the wall to a unique situation where a bride could pass judgment on the rest of her friends and family without anyone knowing. Almost all the comments were flattering. Brides were rarely bitchy on their wedding day, as these guests were all friends and family and they had mostly all made an effort to look good for the special day. Occasionally there would be a sly dig at a particular outfit, hat or hairdo, but it was mostly all light-hearted.

The only exception was if one of the guests arrived wearing what many consider to be the biggest crime possible at a wedding. A white dress. Unless specifically asked by the bride, then it is severely frowned upon for anyone other than the bride to wear white. In those instances, all hell broke loose behind that curtain.

Some people will argue – probably those heretics who choose to wear white – that the bride will stand out from the crowd, regardless of what she wears, or what anyone else is wearing. They also suggest that it's a bit self-important for a bride to expect to be the centre of attention and to have an influence on what other people wear to her wedding. Of course she is being self-important. It's her wedding day!

I saw a lot of non-bridal white dresses at weddings over the years. Unless they were ones requested by the bride – coordinated bridesmaids, for example – they were as welcome as a turd in a swimming pool. Mothers and mothers-in-laws were occasionally the culprits. I always found it very bizarre – and extremely amusing – when they arrived in a white outfit, as though they were making a very public statement that it was their special day too.

The worst case I ever saw was with the new girlfriend of a best man. Neither the bride nor any of the guests had ever met her before, and I got the impression the groom had only met her on a couple of occasions before the wedding. She certainly made an impact from the moment she arrived. She was strikingly beautiful, with long blonde hair, a fantastic figure and perfect skin. She was smiley, charming and charismatic, and I'm certain would have been well loved by all of those at the wedding. Except she arrived wearing a white dress. And before she had even opened her mouth, she became the most hated woman at the wedding. There was no coming back from that. I doubt she would ever have been able to win them over.

Matt and his best man take their place at the front of the church, and the ushers do their ushering. The friends and family file in through the door and I wait outside for Jen's arrival. Jen's mum and the three bridesmaids have just been dropped off, and the car has headed back for Jen and her dad. I stay a good distance down the church path and take some candid photos with my long lens of them all waiting nervously for Jen at the church gate.

After another five minutes, the car comes back into view. Jen's wedding car is a modern Mercedes, owned by Jen's dad. It's not a particularly extravagant wedding car, but it does the job perfectly. Jen's dad's friend is acting as the driver and he has even been bought a special peaked chauffeur cap to look the part. The ribbon attached to the front grill – tied expertly by Jen's dad during his hideout in the garage – makes it unmistakeable as a wedding car.

Unless the bride is getting married at the same place in which she is getting ready, or is within easy walking distance, then some form of transport will be required to get to the ceremony venue. This can come in many forms. Often – as in Jen's case – the bride will just arrive in a car owned by a family member or friend. But I've also seen arrivals at weddings in horse and carts, stretch limousines, convertible sports cars, the back of a pickup truck, a motorbike, a canal boat, a tractor, an NYPD cop car and a helicopter.

Rachel wasn't bothered at all about what car she arrived at the church in for our wedding. She was more than happy for her dad to drive her in his VW Passat. I suggested to Rachel that her dad might not want to be a designated driver on the day of his daughter's wedding, so we looked into alternatives. I had a friend with an old beat-up VW campervan which he was willing to drive us in. It fitted the bill perfectly; it was big and roomy – allowing space for bridesmaids and Rachel's dad – and certainly had character.

When we mentioned our plans to Rachel's parents, they were less than impressed. They had been extremely supportive of all our wedding plans up until this point and had never voiced any objections or criticisms. But when the idea of a rusty old campervan was mentioned, they seemed to be personally offended.

'You can't turn up at the church in that,' said Rachel's mum, when we showed them a photo.

'Why not?' said Rachel.

'Look at it! It would probably break down before you even got to the church.'

'Your mum's right,' said her dad. 'You need to hire a proper wedding car. It's traditional.'

'But wedding cars cost a lot of money. We could use this campervan for free.'

'Don't worry about the money. We want to pay for it.'

So, the following week, Rachel went to a wedding show in Northampton to look at cars. Unfortunately, I couldn't make it because Abington Stanley FC were a player short. What were the chances? My team needed me yet again.

There were lots of different wedding car companies exhibiting at the fair, offering cars to suit all budgets, so Rachel had plenty to choose from. Her parents had not specified what type of car they thought she should hire, only that it should be classic and vintage, rather than something modern.

Perusing through a catalogue from one of the firms, Rachel found a small brown car on the back page. It was cute, simple, kind of dull, and very brown. It was also the cheapest car Rachel had seen for hire by some distance. She phoned me after the match (we lost 7-0) to tell me she had booked it, paid the deposit, and hoped I didn't mind. Of course I didn't mind. It was one more item ticked off our to-do list, and we were keeping the in-laws happy at the same time.

Or so we thought.

When Rachel showed her parents the picture of the car we had hired, they were more disappointed than they had been about the campervan.

'What is THAT?' said Rachel's dad.

'I don't know exactly,' said Rachel. 'But I think it's cute, don't you?'

'That's not a proper wedding car,' said Rachel's mum.

'Yes, it is! It was being advertised at a wedding fair.'

'Isn't it a brown Skoda? It looks more like a funeral car. We can't have you going to your wedding in that.'

'But I've already paid the deposit.'

We hoped that would be enough to end the discussion, but Rachel's parents didn't want to accept the decision. In the end, Rachel phoned the car company to try and 'upgrade' the brown piece of crap we had hired to something more special. Unfortunately, everything else was booked on our wedding day, but after a bit of sweet-talking, they agreed to refund our deposit and we were back to the drawing board.

After many discussions and visits to different car hire companies – I did attend most of these appointments because they weren't on a Sunday morning – we eventually settled on a big, fancy, 'traditional' wedding car. I can remember most things about our wedding – the people, the speeches, the key moments of the day, the emotions – but I only have a very vague recollection of what our car looked like. It was one of the more expensive elements of our day, but it had very little impact on our wedding for me. I have had to flick through our wedding album to remind myself what colour it was. It turns out it was a cream coloured 1927 Rolls Royce Phantom.

Looking back, it was a spectacular car, and I can understand what Rachel's parents saw in it. I feel bad for not appreciating what a privilege it was to be in such an incredible vehicle. But I had just got married to the love of my life, and was on my way to the wedding reception, where I would be surrounded by my closest friends and family for the rest of the day. The quality of the vehicle I was travelling in was not particularly high on my list of priorities. I'm ashamed to say it was not even on my radar at all.

When we had driven the 1.5 miles to the ceremony venue – a journey of about five minutes – Rachel and I thanked the driver and made our way into the marquee. When Rachel's parents arrived at the venue shortly after us, they posed for photos in front of our car for ten minutes. To them, the car was an important part of the day. It was a symbol of a perfect wedding and I'm sure they felt it was worth every penny.

At the time I deeply regretted spending their money on such an opulent and unnecessary car, but, looking back, I'm sort of glad we did. I am sure there were plenty of elements to our wedding that Rachel's mum and dad felt like we were wasting money on, but they chose to keep quiet, understanding that it was our wedding. It is all about compromise. And keeping the in-laws happy.

As with our own wedding, I didn't pay too much attention to the vehicles that the bride or groom arrived at the ceremony in during the weddings I photographed. I would obviously get shots of the car arriving, but my focus was always on the door (not literally, that would result in a really rubbish photo), waiting for the arrival of the most important people.

There were some instances when the choice of transport would arouse my interest. I photographed one wedding where the groom arrived by helicopter. It seemed a little over-the-top at first, and, if I'm honest, slightly knobbish. But, after speaking to the groom, I learned that it had been a surprise for him, booked by the bride, and the smile on his face – which his bride wasn't even there to witness – was priceless.

I have also seen the groom and his groomsmen arrive at the church in a replica A-Team van, which was a little weird but kind of cool. I have seen several horse and carts - which were fun, but a little slow, smelly and unpredictable - and a bride sitting on hay bales in the back of a pickup truck was a particularly novel way to travel.

But my all-time favourite was a groom who arrived at the ceremony in a classic MG. I didn't think anything of the car when it pulled into the venue's driveway, until I noticed the look on the faces of the groomsmen and the parents of both the bride and groom who had assembled outside the venue to meet him. There was a lot of attention being shown to the car, with several of them stroking the bonnet, bumpers and headlights, followed by lots of prolonged hugs with the groom, particularly from the bride's parents. The bride was already inside the venue getting ready, so did not witness any of this strange outpouring of emotion towards her groom and his car.

I learned that the MG used to belong to the bride's grandad, who had died a few years previously. The car had rusted away, was undriveable, and ready for the scrapheap. The groom – a trained mechanic – had spent the last year secretly restoring the car during his lunchbreak at work as a surprise for his new wife. It was a thing of beauty and an incredibly thoughtful and wonderful gesture. And not only did they have a fantastic car to use for the wedding day, but they had the car – along with its memories of her grandad – to cherish forever. The bride's reaction when she saw it after the wedding ceremony was one of the most emotional moments of any wedding I ever photographed.

Jen looks calm and composed as her dad helps her from the car. Her mum steps forward and gives her a final hug, before rushing ahead to take her place in the church.

I take a few photos of Jen with her dad and bridesmaids and then allow Reverend David to assemble them in order outside the church door. I sneak inside and take my place, tucked away at the edge of the transept.

The church organist strikes her first chord, and it sends shivers through my body. No other instrument has such unique power as a church organ. Reverend David glides down the aisle – his long robes hiding his feet – and takes his place at the front.

Then the familiar tune of *Here Comes the Bride* booms through the building. *The Bridal Chorus*, as it is officially known, is a piece of music filled with love and joy that should bring with it nothing but positive emotions. Unfortunately, my feelings towards it changed when a vicar once told me the origin of the music. It was composed by Richard Wagner in 1850 as part of his opera Lohengrin. In the story, the music is played as two newlyweds, Lohengrin and Elsa, proceed to the bedroom to consummate their marriage. It would be an understatement to suggest that Lohengrin and his new wife Elsa don't have the most successful of marriages. In fact, as far as marriages go, it is one of the most catastrophic possible. Shortly after reaching their bed chamber, Lohengrin kills a man, then leaves his new wife Elsa, who soon dies alone from her grief. Apart from that association, The Bridal Chorus is a really romantic piece of music.

A popular Northampton pianist, who played at many weddings I photographed, used to entertain guests with his rendition of The Imperial March – Darth Vader's theme from Star Wars – just before the arrival of the bride. It never failed to break the tension.

Jen and her father enter the church and the congregation all turn to face her. Matt keeps his gaze directed at the floor. He's been told to wait until Reverend David gives him the signal. I can see him take a deep breath to try and compose himself. James, his best man, standing alongside him, gives him a gentle nudge to reassure him that it's all going to be ok.

I step forwards slightly, so that I can get a better view as Jen walks down the aisle. She looks stunning, and her smile is spread wide across her face as she moves her eyes from side to side, trying to take in as many of her friends and family as possible. Then, as she's halfway down the aisle, her gaze turns to Matt at the front. At this point, Reverend David gives Matt a nod and he turns to face his bride. I can see how he visibly gulps and then, as Jen's smile grows even wider, Matt wipes away a tear. Every person in the room is looking at these two and it's impossible not to get caught up in the moment. I too get a little teary. I step back into the shadows as Jen and her father come and stand alongside Matt.

A marriage ceremony, even when stripped back to its basics as the union of two people, has undergone many changes throughout the course of history. Despite the forward-thinking Greeks and Romans embracing same-sex partnerships, it took much of the modern world until the 21st century to legalise same-sex marriage. Most religious institutions still argue and oppose it today, despite the whole concept of marriage pre-dating organised religion.

The legality of different unions has changed many times over the centuries, too. Now almost universally prohibited, sibling marriage was considered quite normal in Roman Egypt – especially amongst the nobility. In the case of Laodice IV, a Greek princess and later leader of the Seleucid Empire in 196 BC, she was married three times to three different kings. Each one was her brother.

Governments have also relaxed their rules on marriage when it suited their political agenda. Polygamy was encouraged in an act of parliament in Nüremberg in 1650 due to a huge shortage of men following the brutal 30 Years War. Men were permitted to marry up to ten women to help with the population imbalance. It is even claimed that during this time men under 60 were forbidden from becoming monks or taking vows of celibacy. In 2001, polygamy was actively encouraged by Omar Hassan al-Bashir, the President of Sudan, to try and accelerate the country's economic development.

And what is considered normal or traditional in one country, might be considered a little unorthodox in others. Take, for example, the 3000-year-old custom of ghost marriages, which are still practised in some parts of China. A ghost marriage is performed when either the bride or groom (or both) are deceased.

Ghost marriages historically involved two dead people. The idea was that although the two people died unmarried, they could be paired up for eternity, and a family bond could be secured. A ceremony took place, followed by a banquet where gifts exchanged hands. Then, to seal the marriage, the grave of the bride would be dug up and her bones placed into the groom's.

In more recent times, ghost marriages have been adapted to allow just one of either the bride or groom to be deceased. These types of marriages are performed for a variety of reasons.

Sometimes, if a fiancé dies before they had a chance to marry then this would be an alternative. These marriages often serve to unite families or secure an heir and continue the family lineage. There is a huge amount of social pressure on people in China to marry and remaining unmarried is considered unnatural. Unmarried men are referred to as 'guang gun' – bare branches – as they are unable to extend the family tree. Unmarried women are known as 'sheng nu' – leftover women – and the names of unmarried daughters cannot be displayed on plaques at the family shrine. Therefore, finding a partner – even if they are already dead, or you are already dead – relieves this social stigma for the family.

Marriages are not always between two humans, whether they are alive or dead. In 2006, a Sudanese man named Charles Tombe was caught having sex with a goat. As punishment, he was forced to marry the goat and even pay a 15,000-dinar dowry. The goat – nicknamed Rose – unfortunately died a year later after choking on a plastic bag. Perhaps she chose to take her own life after the humiliation of being married to a human.

Even more recently, a Balinese teenage boy was forced to marry a cow after being caught having sex with it. In the boy's defence, he did claim that the cow had given him the eye and was trying to flirt with him. During the ceremony, 18-year-old Ngurah Alit succumbed to the humiliation and fainted. The poor innocent cow – or should that be, the evil temptress cow – was drowned in the sea as her punishment. Alit's clothes were drowned in the sea too, in a symbolic act to cleanse the village of the incident, but leaving poor Alit without his new bovine wife, or any clothes.

Reverend David says a few words and then we launch into a couple of hymns. Jen and Matt have gone with two classics – *All*

Things Bright and Beautiful and *Jerusalem*. Unless most of your guests are regular churchgoers, it's best to go with popular hymns, otherwise you will end up with a tangle of many different melodies from the clueless congregation. I enjoy being a guest at a wedding, christening, church concert or funeral and seeing a hymn that I have never heard before. It's great fun trying to blag your way through a song when you have no bloody clue how it goes. Rachel usually stands alongside me silently cringing as I belt out my own rendition of a tune I am hearing for the very first time.

'Who gives this woman to be married to this man?' says Reverend David.

'I do,' says Jen's dad.

The father giving away his daughter is still a key symbolic part of the wedding. Because of the diversity of modern family situations, with divorced parents, step-fathers, fathers that have passed away, or absent fathers, brides are often nowadays given away by mothers, multiple fathers, brothers or friends. Sometimes brides choose to walk down the aisle alone and not be given away by anyone.

Some people consider a father giving away his daughter an outdated and chauvinistic tradition. It suggests ownership of the bride and implies that the wedding is a business transaction. That's because the act of a father giving away his daughter was exactly that. The daughter was considered to be the property of the father, and passing his daughter's hand from his to her husband's would be the formal sealing of a deal – often involving land, money, family unity or a combination of all three. All fathers tend to look uncomfortable during this part of the ceremony, and I'm not sure it does much to promote feminism and female independence.

Jen's dad does what is requested of him, though, and Jen is formally passed over to Matt where she now stands to his left. The bride always stands to the groom's left. That's the way it has always been (apart from Jewish weddings where the bride traditionally stands on the right). Like many other wedding officiants, Reverend David likes to include a mention of the origin of this tradition in his service.

'There is a very special reason why the groom always stands on the bride's right,' he says. 'Does anybody know?'

'*I DO!*' I want to shout, but I stay quiet.

There's a small murmuring from the congregation, but nobody responds. I don't think Reverend David actually wants anyone to respond. This isn't an audience participation bit.

'Well…' he goes on, 'The reason the groom stands to the bride's right is so that he has his sword arm free to protect her.'

Jen and Matt smile and the rest of the congregation laugh, and then the wedding continues. This reason given by Reverend David, and wedding officiants across the world, is true. But it only tells part of the story. If the full story was told, it might make the tradition seem more than a little sordid and pose some serious questions about why we still stick to it.

The groom having his sword arm free to protect his wife sounds extremely brave, gallant and romantic. But the truth is that the bride had often been kidnapped by the groom, against her will. He needed his sword arm free so he could fend off the bride's family and friends who were trying to steal her back, before he could force her into marriage. See? It's not so brave, gallant and romantic now.

The practise of the bride standing on the left is out-dated, derogatory and sexist. It demeans women, but more importantly, it is extremely insulting to left-handed grooms.

SEVEN

Most weddings will have at least one reading during the ceremony. It's a chance for your chosen friend or family member to express some sentiments about love or marriage in front of the rest of your guests. But mostly, readings are just a way of padding out your wedding service to make it feel more of an event.

You should use it as a chance to have something read that has meaning to you as a couple. An extract from a favourite book or film perhaps, or even a song. At our wedding, my uncle read the lyrics to The Proclaimers' *I'm Gonna Be (500 Miles)* in the church (with a few of the congregation whispering the '*ba-da-ba-baa*'s), and it went down really well.

I do have one piece of advice for you. Do NOT have someone read *A Lovely Love Story* by Edward Monkton. You probably know the poem. It's about two dinosaurs falling in love, and one of them being keen on shopping and the other being fond of 'things'. People seem to love it and it has become incredibly popular as a wedding reading since it was published. It's because it's so wacky and random and 'out there'. It is also a load of absolute horseshit, and it makes me irrationally angry whenever I hear it. When you listen to it read at a wedding for the first time, you think '*ha, this is different. A reading about dinosaurs going shopping? That's so wacky and random and 'out there.'* When you listen to it read at a wedding for the fiftieth time, you want to run to the front of the room and punch the reader's face in. I was just one wedding away from acting on this desire. It's a ridiculously stupid story and deserves no place in any wedding.

Sorry, Edward, I love all your other stuff, just not that wacky dinosaur crap.

Thankfully Jen and Matt don't choose *A Lovely Love Story* by Edward Monkton. If they had, my final wedding would have ended with me physically assaulting a member of the public in a place of worship. As it is, they have a couple of standard Bible readings and an extract from *Captain Corelli's Mandolin*, which is read out at every wedding that doesn't feature *A Lovely Love Story*. Despite hearing it dozens of times, I actually like the reading from Louis de Bernieres' book. It's the passage about love – unsurprisingly – and the differences between love and being in love. *'Love itself is what is left over when being in love has burned away'*. It's a nice sentiment and strikes the right chord between being gushy but not too puke-inducing.

Another popular wedding reading – which my mum read at our wedding – is an extract of *The Prophet* by Kahlil Gibran called *Thoughts on Marriage*. It seemed ok at the time, but looking back it's a bit dull and depressing. It's all about being one with your partner but remaining your own person. What it really needed was some dinosaurs going shopping to liven it up a bit.

Kahlil Gibran's *The Prophet* would not be allowed in a civil ceremony because it mentions the G-word. God. *The Marriage and Registration Act* of 1856 stated that registry office marriages could not contain religious content. Even as recently as 1995, the act went one step further by amending the wording to state: *'Any reading, music, words or performance which forms part of a ceremony of marriage celebrated on the premises must be secular in nature'*. This was relaxed slightly in 2005 when the act was amended to allow an incidental reference to God, providing it was in a non-religious context.

And that ruling still applies today. Khalil Gibran's reference to God is considered religious – *'you shall be together even in the silent memory of God'* – and is likely to be forbidden in a civil ceremony. However, if you want to have the lyrics to *Funky Shit* by The Prodigy read at your wedding, then go right ahead. The song's entire lyrics consist of the line *'Oh my god that's the funky shit.'* I think it's safe to say that despite the multiple mentions of the word god, the meaning of the song is unlikely to be considered religious in nature. But maybe I'm wrong. I am disappointed I have never heard it read during any wedding I've ever been to.

I had couples who were not allowed to have Robbie Williams' *Angels* played at the end of their ceremony because of the deemed 'religious nature'. I had another couple who wanted to read the more traditional marriage vows of *'for richer for poorer, in sickness and in health, 'til death us do part'* during their civil ceremony but were not allowed due to its association with religion. It seems absurd and petty that these rules still apply and that such a strict line must be drawn between religious and civil wedding ceremonies.

If you are getting married in a church, most vicars will insist (or politely suggest) that at least one of your readings is a Bible reading. I understand that it makes sense to respect the book that the entire church is based on, rather than substitute it for a less religious reading, such as *Funky Shit* by The Prodigy. There are a small handful of Bible readings that pop up at most church weddings, partly because very few people know the Bible well enough to be able to pick another relevant passage and so turn to tried and tested readings, but mostly because the Bible actually says very little about marriage.

The most popular Bible reading at weddings is *1 Corinthians 13:4-8: 'Love is patient, love is kind. It does not envy, it does not boast, it is not proud'*. I like it. It's a nice verse, and Rachel and I had it read at our wedding. But it's not about marriage. There are very few passages in the Bible that do mention marriage, and those that do are a little vague.

Reverend David mentions in his sermon how Jesus was a guest at a wedding in Cana of Galilee. This 'fact' is even included in the standard welcome for most church wedding ceremonies – as though Jesus being a guest at a wedding somehow ties the whole idea of marriage closer to the church and to God. Is that really the best they can do? Most people have been a guest at a wedding. Often many weddings. So Jesus was a guest at a wedding? Big deal! I've been to hundreds of weddings, so presumably that makes me infinitely more of a sage about marriage than Jesus? Ok, admittedly Jesus did make quite an impression at the wedding he attended in Cana of Galilee as it was the occasion he first performed the miracle of turning water into wine. That's quite a trick, I'll give him that, but it doesn't really provide valuable evidence of the links between God and marriage.

Jesus chose not to marry. In fact, he openly encouraged people not to marry and asked them to follow him instead. In Matthew 19:29 he says: '*And everyone who has left houses or brothers or sisters or father or mother or wife or children or fields for my sake will receive a hundred times as much and will inherit eternal life*'. He seems to be offering a pretty substantial reward – it doesn't get much bigger than eternal life – for people to follow him, instead of devoting their life to their home or family. Paul, one of Jesus's apostles (although not one of the famous 12), also encouraged Christians, 'do not take a wife.' Vicars surprisingly don't tend to quote these passages during wedding sermons.

The Bible says very little about marriage, but some of what it does say is quite disturbing. For example, it says that if a man marries a woman and then accuses her of not being a virgin, the father of the bride is summoned and must prove his daughter's virginity (however that might be). If the man is wrong, he gets whipped, fined and then must stay with his wife for the rest of his life and is forbidden from ever divorcing her. If, however, it turns out he was right and she wasn't a virgin, she gets stoned to death. Or there is the bit in *Deuteronomy* that says how rape victims are forced to marry their rapist. Weirdly, I never saw either of these Bible passages chosen as wedding readings either.

The reason that marriage and weddings do not feature prominently in the Bible, is because marriage and religion have not always been so entwined. Marriages, throughout most of history, served a civil purpose and ceremonies to bond people simply took place to unite families, solve disputes, secure heirs and provide stability. It wasn't until the 12th century that the Roman Catholic Church began referring to marriage as a sacrament, and another 400 years until it was officially declared one. Considering the first recorded evidence of marriage was in 2350 BC – with ceremonies uniting people having taken place for thousands of years before that – that's incredibly slow for the church to get in on the act.

To be fair to the church, when marriage and religion did finally form a recognised union, the church did improve the concept of marriage, and helped begin an important transition for the roles of men and women, taking a big step towards the sacred union of today's partnerships.

From my position, perched on a pew in the transept, I have a full view of Jen, and I can see the right side of Matt's face as they face each other. A beam of sunlight shines through one of the upper stained-glass windows, backlighting Jen's dress beautifully. Her veil, billowing around her head and shoulders, diffuses the light perfectly, allowing me some stunning shots as they say their vows. Jen's veil is not covering her face. Veils are still popular, but few brides seem to go for the face veil these days and instead wear it as a hair accessory.

The veil is one of the oldest surviving wedding accessories that is still used today, perhaps only predated by the wedding ring. The earliest documented reference to the veil comes from about 1400BC in the Middle Assyrian Empire. Veils came to symbolise virginity and innocence of the bride, with the groom being the first to 'uncover' her. Later, ancient Romans and Greeks used the veil as a way to ward off evil spirits. Then, through centuries of arranged marriages, the veil became another layer of disguise for the bride, so that the groom could not do a runner until it was too late.

Reverend David begins Jen and Matt's declaration to each other. This is the part where they say, '*I do*', or more commonly, '*I will*' (but the word 'will' doesn't fit so easily in diamantes on the sole of a shoe). But before he begins, he says the line:

'First, I am required to ask anyone present who knows a reason why these persons may not lawfully marry, to declare it now.' In civil ceremonies, the registrar will ask if anyone knows of '*any lawful impediment*'.

This is perhaps one of the most dreaded parts of the wedding day. It is the bit that you often see in films, TV soaps or adverts, when someone bursts through the door at the back of the church and declares their undying love to either the bride or groom. Only, it never happens in real life. Well, not in any of the weddings I photographed anyway.

The reason why this doesn't happen in real life is because declaring your undying love to someone does not constitute a legal reason for a couple not to get married. Even if the love was reciprocated from one of those getting married, that does not qualify as a legal reason for the wedding to not go ahead. Even if the person who burst into the church had been sleeping with either the bride or groom (or both) for many years – that still does not count. If such a scenario occurred, it would be up to the bride and groom to decide if the wedding should continue. In the eyes of God or the law, nothing has been said that should stop the wedding from proceeding.

A couple don't have to love each other to get married. They don't even have to pretend. There is no test to see if a couple actually like each other – perhaps there should be, although I'm not sure what that would entail.

So, under what circumstances can a wedding be called off?

A wedding can be called off for only a few very specific reasons. It cannot legally continue if it is believed the bride or groom is mentally incapacitated, meaning they don't know what they are doing. Alcohol-induced incapacitation is also a valid reason. There was one particularly scary registrar whom I worked with regularly, who used to seek out the groom in the venue's bar before every wedding and tell him that the wedding would not legally be able to go ahead if he was in the least bit drunk, at which point the groom would look panic-stricken and put down his pint.

'It would not be the first time I've had to call off a wedding,' she would say, striding away from the bar.

I once asked the registrar about this in private. Had she really ever had to call off a wedding because of the groom being a little bit tipsy?

'No, of course not,' she said. 'I just say that to scare them a little and make them behave a bit more responsibly.'

A wedding can also be called off if it turns out that either the bride or groom is already married. The onus is on the person making the objection, so they would have to prove the accusation they were making.

Another cause for a wedding to be called off is if it transpires that either of the couple is underage. Again, this must be proven by the objector and checks have usually been made by the vicar or registrar beforehand to ensure this doesn't happen.

As well as regularly being asked for ID when buying glue, Rachel was also asked for ID from the vicar that married us. This was not as a formality to prove her name and address, but to provide evidence she was actually over the legal age. When we sat down with our vicar to have our initial meeting, he removed his glasses and looked at us very sternly.

'Now, there are only a few reasons why you can't legally get married. One is if either of you is already married.' Rachel and I looked at each other and chuckled. The vicar chuckled too.

'Well I'm not,' I said.

'Neither am I,' said Rachel.

'That's good,' smiled the vicar.

'The other reason, and this applies mostly to you, Rachel, is that you are not old enough.'

Rachel and I looked at each other and chuckled. This time, the vicar didn't chuckle too. In fact, his stare became more intense and he looked suspiciously at Rachel.

Our laughter tailed off when we realised he wasn't joking.

'I'm 25!' said Rachel.

'I am sorry to have to ask, but I have been duped before,' he said, and continued to look accusingly at me and Rachel. The legal age to marry in the UK is 16, with parents' consent, and as the vicar knew our parents would be involved with the wedding, he was suggesting Rachel was under 16. As flattering as it was for Rachel to be a 25-year-old still looking like an under-16, it was a double-whammy of insults for me. Firstly, there was no question that he thought I looked old. But he was also indirectly accusing me of being a paedophile.

'She's 25!' I said.

'I'm sorry, but it's Rachel I need to hear this from.' His expression towards Rachel then changed from suspicion to sympathy. As if offering her a chance to escape this child-trafficker she was being forced to marry. I clocked this look and took it personally.

'She's two months older than me!' I blurted.

'Rachel, is this true?' he said, not believing a word I said.

'Yes, it's true. I am older.'

'See, I told you!' I said, 'I'm basically her toy boy.'

'Alright George, you can stop now,' said Rachel, as she delved into the depths of her handbag. 'Here's my driving licence.'

He studied it carefully, a look of astonishment on his face, and then handed it back.

'25! Well I never. So, have you thought about which hymns you would like during the service?' he said, and the paedophile accusations were forgotten.

A wedding can also not go ahead if it turns out that either the bride or groom are not who they say they are. This came agonisingly close to happening at the wedding of Luke and Suzi. Their wedding was a civil ceremony in a picturesque manor house in Sussex. I had photographed the bridal preparations at Suzi's parents' house in the morning and then arrived at the venue to get some photos of Luke and his groomsmen. They had a quick beer at the bar and then I took photos of them all in the grounds of the venue before Luke was called in to see the registrar for his pre-wedding interview. In civil ceremonies in the UK, it is a requirement for both the bride and groom to each have an interview with the registrar immediately before the ceremony to basically prove their identity and check everything is in order.

These meetings tend to last ten minutes at most, but twenty had passed and Luke was still shut in the room with the registrar. Following the interview, the groom is usually ushered quickly into the ceremony room, and then the bride goes through for her interview, ensuring their paths don't cross. Luke's bride, her bridesmaids, and her parents arrived at the venue in their car and the groom was still in the office. The best man, who had gone to check everything was ok, emerged from the room looking flustered.

'There have been a few complications,' he said.

'What sort of complications?' I asked.

'It's to do with Luke's name.' At this point I saw a glimmer of a smile on the best man's face. 'I'll explain later. He's such a dick,' he said, shaking his head. 'We need to get Suzi to wait outside for a bit longer.'

We made up some excuse to the bride about there being a delay, whilst reassuring her that everything was fine and there was absolutely nothing to worry about.

Thankfully the matter was soon resolved. Luke – who had earlier seemed like one of the coolest and most relaxed grooms I had ever seen – emerged from the room, sweating profusely, red-cheeked and looking incredibly stressed. He breathed a physical sigh of relief, managed a brief smile towards me, and then hurried into the ceremony room.

The bride's interview went without a hitch and the wedding ceremony went ahead as planned, but 20 minutes later than scheduled.

Later that day I found out the cause of the delay.

While on the stag do, Luke and his friends had spent a day drinking in some eastern European city. During the evening, the conversation moved onto middle names. For some unknown reason, Luke told all his friends that his middle name was Hercule.

'No it's not,' they all laughed.

'It is,' said Luke adamantly.

'No. It's not,' said the best man. 'Mate, I've known you nearly my whole life and I think I would have known if your middle name was Hercule.'

'You never asked.'

'Asked if your middle name was Hercule? Why would I ask that?'

'No, asked me what my middle name was.'

'I'm sure I did. Anyway, it would have come up at some point. Your middle name is NOT Hercule.'

'It is,' said Luke.

'No it's not. I bet you £20 it isn't.'

'Fine,' said Luke, shaking his best man's hand.

The groom's middle name was not Hercule. He didn't even have a middle name. But he had always so desperately wanted one. So, when he got home from the stag do, he decided to give himself a middle name. He decided to give himself the middle name Hercule.

He paid to have his name officially changed by deed poll and then had his passport and driving licence amended to show his new name. He even had a framed certificate made of his official name change that he had planned to present to the best man during his wedding speech. He couldn't wait to see the look on his best man's face when he showed him – hoping it would be enough to win the bet.

Only, he didn't quite anticipate how much of a problem this new middle name would cause for the bureaucracy associated with weddings. When he and his fiancée had filled in all the paperwork for their wedding, and attended the various meetings with the registry office, he didn't have the middle name Hercule. And on his birth certificate that he had provided at the time, he didn't have the middle name Hercule. But when he had gone to his pre-wedding interview with the registrar and he had been asked to provide some identification, he suddenly had this mysterious new middle name.

The registrar initially said that the wedding could not go ahead. Much discussion and begging followed, and eventually after a long phone call with some Super Senior Registrar, they were able to iron out the technicalities and allow the wedding to proceed.

Another wedding was booked at the ceremony venue soon after theirs and so the wedding was almost called off due to the delay potentially impacting the next wedding. As a compromise, we agreed to do a minimal number of photos at the ceremony venue and save them for the reception.

After it had all been sorted out, the registrar seemed to see the funny side, and she read out his full name during the service with a deadly serious voice. There were huge guffaws from all those present on the stag do when the name 'Hercule' was read out and looks of shock and confusion from the rest of the guests – including the groom's family, and his new wife.

The groom and best man both told bits of the story during their speeches, allowing the wedding guests to share the joke too. And the best man – true to his word – paid up the bet.

Nobody speaks up or bursts in through the door when Reverend David asks if anyone knows of any reason why Jen and Matt should not be married. They both turn and look at their guests and smile, the congregation all snigger, and then Matt does a mock wiping of his brow.

It's almost time for Jen and Matt to be pronounced husband and wife and to share their first married kiss. The Bible says, '*a man shall leave his father and mother and be joined to his wife, and the two shall become one flesh',* and it is claimed by some Christians that the kiss symbolises the moment that the bride and groom become *one flesh.* I'm no theologian, but I'm pretty sure the Bible is actually referring to a different type of physical union of '*one flesh*' in this passage. But I can understand that it is a bit impractical to suggest a bride and groom end their wedding ceremony by becoming one flesh at the front of the church in front of everyone.

It is more likely that the kiss was used, like the father passing his daughter's hand to her groom, as a way of sealing the deal in the marriage contract. The kiss is still a pivotal moment in most weddings. However, it is surprisingly omitted from many marriage ceremonies. I am never quite sure whether this is to do with the personal reservations of the couple, or a particularly prudish vicar, but it always leaves the ceremony feeling unfinished.

Reverend David announces Jen and Matt's kiss with great enthusiasm, and Matt doesn't even hesitate before putting both his hands around Jen's waist and pulling her towards him. She throws her arms around the back of his neck and they hold a very passionate kiss for several seconds, before turning their heads to the congregation who are all whooping and cheering. They kiss each other again, the cheers get louder, and then they take each other's hands and turn back to face the beaming Reverend David.

So that was it. The last time I will ever photograph two people getting married. Until now, I had just been swept along by the day as usual, but as the bridal party are ushered through to the vestry to sign the register, I look out at the congregation and realise that I am truly going to miss this. I sit back in my pew and take a few deep breaths, trying to savour the moment.

I capture a few wide-angled photos of the church and then make my way through to the vestry to join the others for the signing of the register.

Very few vicars or registrars will allow the photographer to take photographs during the signing of the register. This is partly due to it being an important moment and the couple won't want the distraction of the camera shutter or flash. But the main reason is that each double-page spread of the marriage register contains personal information such as names, addresses and occupations, not just of the couple getting married, but up to three other couples – plus their parents and witnesses. Never mind that all this information is available in an online search of marriage registers, inside the church it is considered top-secret information.

Instead, the vicar or registrar will wait for everyone to sign the register and then they will either bring out a dummy book, or flick to a blank page, and the bride and groom then have to sit and pretend to sign the book again while the photographer gets their photos.

Reverend David knows that I must not, under any circumstances, take any photos during the signing of the register. He knows it is his duty to tell photographers this. But he doesn't seem to know why. The same happens with many other officiants; they bark orders and keep a close eye on me to make sure I don't even think about taking a photo during the signing of the register. I've photographed enough weddings to know that's it's really not worth it, so I don't even raise my camera. Nothing exciting ever happens during the signing of the register anyway. Then, after being happy that I have not taken any sneaky photos, they allow me to come forward to take some posed photos. But – as Reverend David is doing now – they leave the original marriage register in front of the couple, on the actual page they signed, with all the other 'top secret' details on full display. As far he is concerned, it means nothing, he just knew I wasn't allowed to take photos while they were signing.

Taking photos of the signing of the register is one of my least favourite parts of the wedding day. As if signing the register isn't boring enough, the couple pretending to sign it again forms the least-natural photograph of the entire wedding. I always try to get this over with as soon as possible so that we can get on with the rest of the day.

I take a few staged photos of Jen and Matt signing and then sneak out of the room and down the aisle to the back of the church. Reverend David assembles the bridal party and then the organist kicks in again with Felix Mendelssohn's *Wedding March*. It's another powerful piece of music, which plays a prominent part in most church weddings. But it was never intended to be played at weddings. It was written for a production of *A Midsummer Night's Dream* in 1842 and, given the pagan nature of Shakespeare's play, seems somewhat out of place in a religious ceremony.

Both Mendelssohn's Wedding March, and Wagner's Bridal Chorus, only became popular features of a wedding after they were used in the wedding of Queen Victoria's eldest daughter – Princess Victoria – during her marriage to Prince Frederick of Prussia in 1858. If only Black Lace's *Do The Conga* had been around at the time. Traditional wedding exits could have been so much better.

The bride and groom's exit from the church is one of my favourite moments of a wedding. It's the first time during their briefly married lives where they look perfectly happy and relaxed together. The stress of the ceremony is behind them and they have a hell of a party to look forward to. They are finally married. This is the start of the rest of their lives.

Jen and Matt squeeze each other's hands tightly as they walk down the aisle, their eyes dancing to friends and family either side of them. I stay where I am towards the back of the church as they turn left and exit into the bright October sun.

EIGHT

Some photographers will whisk the bride and groom away immediately after the ceremony to begin the photos. It is certainly easier to get the formal photographs done as soon as possible, as it then frees up the rest of the day for the couple to enjoy themselves. But I always feel that these first few minutes after the ceremony are a hugely important time for the couple – particularly the bride. The groom will have usually seen most of the guests before the ceremony, but for the bride it will be the first time she will be able to speak to her friends and family. This time is better spent greeting guests than rushing straight into the photos.

St Peter's has a very small churchyard and Jen and Matt have already agreed that we will do the group photos once we get to the reception venue. After people have a glass of champagne in their hands, they are more amiable to standing around waiting for photos.

The church bells sound out high above us as the wedding guests all mingle outside the church for ten minutes. A couple of rebel aunties throw handfuls of confetti over Jen and Matt. Others are hesitant because Reverend David did mention confetti in his address. He told the congregation that he was perfectly happy for guests to throw confetti… providing they throw it outside the church gate. Which means that he is not happy at all about confetti being thrown anywhere near the church. Outside of the gate means it is no longer church property and will likely be the local council's responsibility to clear up, and not his.

Reverend David spots the two dissidents throwing confetti, and rather than speak to them, walks over to me and reminds me that people are not allowed to throw confetti in the church grounds. Vicars and wedding coordinators often do this, as though we photographers are the confetti guardians and should be held directly responsible for instigating any rogue confetti incidents in controlled confetti-free zones. Most churches and wedding venues hate confetti. They accept that it is part of a wedding, but they do everything they can to either prevent or restrict its usage.

Despite being made to feel responsible for these rogue confetti rebels, I know I can get this situation to work in my favour. If someone doesn't encourage guests to leave soon, everyone will be hanging out at this church forever, and Reverend David will gradually lose his shit as his churchyard piles up with confetti. Nobody wants to see that.

I grab the two ushers – Rob and Nathan – and ask them to do the rounds and tell everyone that we are going to do a confetti photo outside the church gate. Guests get very excited about a confetti photo. It's a rare chance for them to acceptably throw something at another person. They've been clutching their handfuls of petals since the end of the ceremony wondering when the right time will be to throw it. That time has come.

The ushers and I encourage all the guests to make two lines either side of the church gate, extending down the road, and ask those with boxes of confetti to donate a handful to anyone without. Then I give the signal to Jen and Matt, who walk between the lines of guests as they get showered with confetti from all angles. Confetti is a fantastic photo opportunity for wedding photographers; it's the perfect combination of colour, action, excitement and joy that can result in some stunning photos.

Jen and Matt reach the end of the line, and their wedding car is waiting for them with the doors already open and they climb in. I look up to see Reverend David smiling and giving me the thumbs up.

'Thank you,' he says.

'No, thank you,' I say, shaking him by the hand.

'Hopefully see you again soon.'

I smile, but don't respond. I haven't told him it is my last wedding. I haven't told anyone.

Where did this tradition of throwing bits of coloured paper at the newlyweds originate?

The custom began in Italy. Fruit, sweets and grains were thrown at festivals as a symbol of something or other – prosperity or fertility probably. The lower classes would often protest about this wastage of good food by throwing rotten eggs or squashed fruit instead – hence the continued Italian tradition of the Battle of the Oranges festival in Ivrea.

Over time, confetti took the form of sugar-coated seeds or nuts, and was later replaced by coloured paper. Next time vicars or venues complain about what a nuisance confetti is, remind them it could have been squashed fruit or rotten eggs instead.

Rice has been thrown at newlyweds for hundreds of years too. The Romans used to throw wheat as a symbol of fertility, and this was later changed to rice because people believed rice symbolised fertility better (No? Me neither). Even today there will often be some old granny at a wedding who will pull out a box of Uncle Ben's from her handbag and start chucking handfuls of the stuff at the bride and groom. If you've ever been hit in the face with a handful of rice, you'll know that it stings like hell. Thankfully, this tradition seems to be on the way out.

Part of the reason for the tradition of rice throwing declining in popularity – particularly in the U.S. – was a series of rumours that began circulating about how dry rice used at weddings was causing the deaths of thousands of birds. It was reported by various sources that after the wedding celebrations had moved on, birds would swoop down and devour all the uncooked rice from the floor. The rice would then swell up in the birds' stomachs and the birds would literally explode.

Stories spread of flocks of exploding birds at weddings all over the world. The hysteria reached such a level that it led to a bill being passed in Connecticut in 1985 making it illegal for uncooked rice to be used in nuptial affairs. The irony was that these stories were all a load of complete and utter bollocks. Despite the rumours, there was not even one single substantiated case of a bird exploding – or even dying – because of uncooked rice. One scientist even did a study and concluded that rice expands in a bird's stomach less than normal birdseed.

Perhaps starting some more unsubstantiated rumours could see the end to other ridiculous wedding traditions. Did you know that 70% of brides who wear a silver sixpence in their shoe develop a permanent limp? Did you know that every couple who have *A Lovely Love Story* by Edward Monkton read during their wedding ceremony will be divorced within six months?

As a caveat, if you are planning on getting married, please use dried petals for your confetti, or at the very least biodegradable and environmentally friendly confetti. Petals will disintegrate to nothing after heavy rain, but even coloured paper will linger for a long time. Not only is it bad for the environment, but it acts as an ugly reminder of the stream of weddings that have passed through that church or venue, making each wedding feel less of a unique occasion.

I poke my head in through the passenger door of Jen and Matt's wedding car. I sometimes need to encourage couples to squash in close together to get a photo in the back of the car, but Jen and Matt are already practically sitting on each other's laps. I take a quick photo.

'Perfect, thank you,' I say. 'Congratulations again. See you at the reception!'

It hasn't always been so easy.

While photographing one of my weddings for Sugar Sweet Precious Memories – the local wedding photography company I did some jobs for – I had one bride who wouldn't allow her groom to get anywhere near her in the wedding car. Arguments between the couple began outside the church, immediately after the ceremony. The couple's three-year-old son – a little shit called Dean – was thirsty and the bottles of water being offered to him by various guests were not adequate. He wanted juice. More importantly, he wanted HIS juice. Rather than telling Dean to stop being such a spoiled little dick, the bride launched an angry tirade at the groom in front of her guests for forgetting to bring Dean's juice.

'I thought you had it,' said the groom.

'How the fuck would I have it? I've been at the hairdresser's all morning. Do you think I had time to worry about a bottle of juice?'

'I've had things to do this morning, too.'

'Like what?'

'Just stuff.'

'You only had one job today and that was to bring Dean's juice. You know how angry he gets.'

I wonder where Dean gets his irrational anger from? I thought.

112

The guests who had filed out of the church stood awkwardly around on the grass, pretending that they couldn't hear or see the newlyweds' argument happening right in front of them.

The bride and groom each put on a fake smile and mingled separately with their guests for 15 minutes until it was time to go to the reception venue. Dean was taken away screaming by the bride's sister, and the not-so-happy couple climbed into the back of a stretch limousine. I leaned in to take a quick photo of the two of them together in the back of the car.

'Smile!' I said, realising this was a long shot.

The groom managed to force a smile as he lifted his arm to put around his bride.

'Get your hands off me!' she snapped, and he quickly put his hand back where it was.

They both forced a grimace; I clicked the shutter, and then got out of that car as quickly as I could.

The reception was an even more uncomfortable affair. It was a big vacuous room at a country club, but it was only about a third full of guests. There were a handful of people sat at each table, and for some reason, none of them seemed to know each other. Dean was still kicking off about his fucking juice. The bride and groom moved separately around the room speaking to guests, and I managed a few forced couple shots and then the bride disappeared upstairs to her bedroom for over an hour until the start of the wedding breakfast, which was the end of my coverage for that wedding.

I had no further follow-up after sending my photos to Sugar Sweet Precious Memories, but I would be very surprised if the couple managed to stay married until the end of the year. I would be surprised if they lasted until the end of their wedding night. Ah, sugar sweet precious memories.

There is a quick toot of the horn and then Jen and Matt's car pulls away. The guests all cheer, and then, from underneath Jen's dad's Mercedes, a pile of tin cans appears and rattles down the road. Rob and Nathan, the ushers, high-five each other.

The custom of tin cans being tied to the back of the wedding car is not as commonplace as it once was. Possibly because of people being more precious about their cars, local authorities being more precious about their roads, and perhaps an overall feeling that dragging the contents of your recycling bin around the countryside is a little bit weird.

There are several theories as to the origin of the tin cans, and it's likely that a combination of all of them led to it becoming a recognised custom. One theory goes back to a time in Tudor England when it was customary for wedding guests to throw their shoes at the bride and groom's carriage after a wedding. A direct hit was believed to bring good luck to the person doing the throwing. Imagine if this was still a wedding tradition today. What a spectacle that would be. So much more fun than confetti! At some point, brides and grooms began objecting to this practice – I can't see why – so shoes were tied to the back of the carriage instead. Unsurprisingly, most guests then instantly regretted giving up their footwear when it dawned on them that they would be barefoot for the rest of the day, so eventually the shoes were somehow replaced with tin cans.

Another theory suggests its origins come from the French custom of *charivari,* practiced since the Middle Ages, which eventually travelled with French settlers to America. Guests would bang pots and pans and create a commotion outside the couple's bedroom – often late at night – and the couple would be expected to come out and feed their hungry guests again. The ungrateful bastards. Over time, guests stopped being so greedy, but continued this *charivari* in the form of tin cans attached to the car.

The final theory states that it was a way to ward off evil spirits for the newlyweds and ensure a happy start to their marriage.

I was 10 when my aunt and uncle married. It was the first wedding I had ever been to and my only previous experience of weddings was from films and television. My overriding memory of these fictional weddings was the decorated car. So, when I was invited to my first wedding, decorating the car became my focus. My aunt and uncle were using their own car to drive from the church, so my sister, cousins and I tied tin cans to the back bumper, wrapped ribbons over the bonnet and wing-mirrors, and then drew a giant love heart and wrote *JUST MARRIED* in shaving foam on the bonnet. I'm sure I had seen that in the movies too.

The following day, when the car had been cleaned off, the heart and the *JUST MARRIED* remained. The shaving foam had reacted with the bonnet and discoloured the paintwork.

We were all very apologetic, and my aunt and uncle were very understanding – and thankfully not too precious about their car – and learned to live with and be proud of their car's new permanent decoration.

Jen and Matt's guests all make their way back to their cars, and I smugly jog back to mine further down the road, knowing I will be able to escape before all of them. It's a ten-minute drive to the reception venue: a beautiful pair of converted barns, surrounding an idyllic courtyard in the Northamptonshire countryside. I have photographed at the venue many times before. It's a fantastic spot, and I can't think of a better place to end my photography career.

The venue will be one of the first things you book for your wedding. Its location, size, style and cost are all important factors that you will obviously weigh up when making your decision.

There are some incredible places to get married out there. And they often come with an eye-watering price tag. It is understandable that you might have your heart set on a particular venue, but don't book your dream venue at the expense of having to trim down your guest list, either because there is not enough space at the venue to include all your guests, or because the cost prohibits you from asking everyone you want. If there are people you want to be at your wedding, but you can't invite them because of the cost of your venue, find a cheaper venue. Your guest list is far more important than your venue.

It's worth remembering that, in my experience, there is no correlation whatsoever between the cost of the venue and the enjoyment factor of the wedding. If anything, I would say the more understated and relaxed the venue, the better the atmosphere.

Pick a venue that suits your personality. Just because you can afford a stupidly over the top location for your wedding, doesn't necessarily mean you should book one. I once photographed a wedding at an extremely opulent stately home. It was a stately home that didn't usually do weddings, but the entire house had been hired for the weekend for a ludicrous sum. I arrived at the venue expecting an extravagant well-to-do couple and was surprised to discover the groom was a down-to-earth builder. He had built up his business from scratch into a multi-million-pound company and wanted to show off his wealth to his friends and family at his wedding.

It was a relatively small wedding, as the house could only seat about 30 people around its table. All the wedding guests were from the same working-class background as the groom before he had made his fortune. Sitting at the long dining room table, being served fine-dining food by silver service, everyone – including the bride and groom, and me – looked very uncomfortable. Yes, it was a wonderful venue, but it was too much for the occasion. They all looked like they would much rather be dancing to cheesy music in the local pub, rather than sipping expensive champagne in the library of a stately home and listening to a string quartet. It was the most expensive wedding I have ever photographed, and also the one most lacking in atmosphere.

Jen and Matt's wedding venue is hired exclusively for them. This venue will regularly host weddings on consecutive days, but they will only ever have one wedding per day. Larger venues will often be able to cater for more than one wedding per day. This is all part of the modern wedding industry and venues must do what they can to succeed. I have no problem with this whatsoever, providing the bride and groom are aware of it before they book. It is always worth double-checking with your venue about whether any other weddings will be taking place on the same day or whether the venue is exclusively yours.

One particular venue that I photographed at regularly could cater for four weddings a day, but the grounds were so vast and the facilities so plentiful that the wedding receptions all took place in different buildings in different corners of the estate. The ceremonies, however – unless the couple were having a church wedding elsewhere – all took place in the same building. A beautiful building it was too, with a high-vaulted glass ceiling and white marble pillars.

The venue was slickly run, and on most occasions a wedding party would have moved onto their reception venue long before another wedding party arrived. Unless, of course, a bride or groom was early, or if the ceremony was delayed for some reason, such as a groom changing his middle name to Hercule.

On a couple of occasions, I photographed the bride and groom walking back down the aisle at the end of the ceremony, deeply in love and looking like the happiest they have ever been. At this particular moment, they are the most important people in the world. And then they exit the building, and the first person they see outside the ceremony room is another bride. Standing there in her long ivory dress and clutching a similar bouquet of flowers, waiting for her turn to get married. Imagine the feeling.

I don't think it's possible to see more contempt in the eyes of two people who have never met before. It's like a Wild West showdown. I have honestly thought – ok, I confess, I've secretly hoped – that two brides were going to start attacking each other and tearing each other's dresses to shreds.

You can see them assessing the competition.

'Is her dress nicer than mine?'

'Who did her hair and makeup?'

'Should I have gone with a tiara too?'

'That bouquet looks a little heavy.'

'I can't believe she's wearing those shoes.'

'What a bitch. I want to tear her face off.'

On these occasions, I would tactfully tell my bride and groom there were much better photo opportunities just around the corner and encourage them and their guests as far away from the other bride as possible.

Surprises like this are not what you want on your wedding day. Another local hotel where I regularly photographed offered one of the cheapest wedding packages in town. It proved a popular deal and the venue was always busy. They had two large function rooms and could host two weddings a day, but both rooms shared the same bar.

The system worked well and every wedding I did there was fun. There was never any competition or rivalry. The venue was honest with their non-exclusivity policy and couples understood they would be sharing the hotel bar with another wedding party and – more often than not – some random hotel guests too.

The brides rarely crossed paths as they tended to stay in their respective function rooms and drinks would be brought to them. The guests from each wedding would mingle at the bar, joined by the shared sense of excitement and celebration that comes with a wedding.

However, getting reportage style photographs of the guests in the bar was a challenge for me, as I had no way of knowing which wedding they were a part of. Occasionally after putting together the couple's wedding album, I would receive a polite note from the bride and groom asking me to remove a picture of a random person on page 57 who was nothing to do with their wedding.

NINE

I am the first to arrive at the venue after Jen and Matt. They are taken through to the barn by the wedding coordinator as this will be the first time they have seen it all set up to their specification. Jen and Matt dropped off all their room and table decorations yesterday and then left the well-briefed staff to do the rest. I leave them to enjoy the moment together and instead get some photos of the outside of the venue while it is quiet.

Over the next ten minutes, the guests park up in the car park and make their way through to the courtyard where they are met with a glass of prosecco. There is another barn – often used for onsite civil ceremonies – which is plenty big enough for all the guests if the weather turns bad, but the sun is out, it's mild and there are still a few hours of daylight left, so most people choose to stay outside.

Jen and Matt emerge from the main barn grinning from ear to ear and begin chatting with their guests. Now that everyone is here, we should make a start with the formal photos.

Group photos are still an important part of the wedding. When weddings were photographed with film, these crucial group shots formed the body of the photography. This section of the day can be time-consuming and has the potential to disrupt proceedings and frustrate the hell out of you. But it doesn't have to. The key is to keep it simple. Don't be worried that Uncle Alan might be upset if he's not included in a separate photo with him and all the other aunts and uncles, or if Kath from your work is not in a group shot with the rest of the sales team. Chances are, they won't care, and if they do care then hopefully they will understand. They can always get a casual selfie with you later in the day.

Here's how to make your group photos as pain free as possible. Stick to my advice and nobody has to suffer.

I recommend doing the group shots as soon as possible during the reception. This is partly to ensure that you don't run out of time before the start of the meal, but mostly to get them over and done with so that you can enjoy the rest of the day.

As I said before, wait until everyone has a drink, because they will be happier standing around when armed with a drink. You can have a table nearby for people to place their drinks on if you would rather those in the photo not be holding a glass.

The most difficult aspect of the group shots is locating all the relevant people you need. So, to make this much easier, start with a big group photo of all your wedding guests. This doesn't have to be a fancily-arranged formal shot. Have the photographer stand on a wall, stepladder, or looking out of an upstairs window, stand alongside your new partner and have all your family and friends gather in a tight group close behind you. At Jen and Matt's wedding, I grab a stepladder from my car and place it at the top of some steps in the courtyard. Jen and Matt stand at the bottom of the steps facing towards me, and all of their guests squash into a big group huddle behind them. It takes only a couple of minutes, and because I am high above them, takes very little arranging and doesn't matter who stands in front of whom. They now have a lovely photo of every single person who is at their wedding.

Not only does this create the perfect record of all of your wedding guests, it also keeps Uncle Alan and Kath from sales happy, as they both know they were included in an official group photo.

From atop my stepladder, I fire off a few photos of Jen and Matt and all their guests. Then, to get an alternative shot, without any additional arranging, I tell everyone to wave a hand in the air on the count of three. I then say the line, 'if you're holding a drink… not that hand.' I started using this line after a crazed mother-in-law once manically showered the bride with her glass of white wine when I asked her to wave. This line almost always got a laugh from the crowd below me, and on the couple of occasions it didn't, I knew I was in for one hell of a boring wedding. Jen and Matt's friends and family do the right thing and humour me with a big laugh. Today's wedding is going to be a goodun.

Next, I ask all the bridal party and the immediate family (parents, siblings and grandparents) to stay nearby as they will be needed for some more photos, and the rest of the wedding guests are free to go and enjoy themselves. Remember, most of your guests HATE having their photo taken, so will be absolutely delighted to be politely told to bugger off.

I then – as quickly and efficiently as possible – work my way through my list of the formal group shots. I requested this list from Jen and Matt in advance and then shuffled it around beforehand into the most manageable order. I would provide couples with a suggested list of about eight formal group shots – all different combinations of the families and bridal party – which covers most bases, and I advised them not to stray too far from this list. Occasionally, couples would send me back an amended list with dozens of additional groups added. I would reply politely telling them I would happily do all the requested photos but that it would take up every minute of their wedding reception, and they wouldn't have a chance to actually speak to their guests or enjoy their day. Most of the time, they would get back to me with a dramatically reduced list. Keep it simple. It might only take a fraction of a second to take a photo, but it's the gathering of the people that takes time. It only needs cousin Jane to have gone off for a cheeky cigarette behind the church, or brother-in-law Ian to have decided that now would be an appropriate time to have a poo before the meal, and suddenly you have spent 20 minutes hunting for crucial guests for one single photo and wasted away your wedding day.

If your photographer is staying into the evening reception, there will be plenty of time to get some informal group shots later. You could round up your old Uni mates, or your primary school friends for a quick snap, without breaking up the day. Or, as is mostly the case – much to my relief – you will be having such a great time later in the day that you realise you couldn't give a shit about having any more photographs taken.

Matt's parents are separated and both have new partners. It is very amicable, and Jen and Matt even pose for a photo with both Matt's parents with their new partners.

There are family politics at almost every wedding, to varying degrees of severity. It is inevitable, given the modern divorce rate, that some parents or family members will have separated, and being in close-proximity once again can potentially pose a few problems.

I have had several situations where I have been warned that a mother and father haven't seen each other, let alone spoken to each other, for many years. I have also had situations where parents have split up and been in the middle of a very messy and complicated divorce at the time of their son or daughter's wedding. I have also photographed weddings where guests had split from their partners in the days leading up to the wedding and it was too late to make any changes to the table plan, and both guests were adamant they were still coming to the wedding.

However complicated and ugly the relationship situation, I have seen it. But what I also noticed, almost without exception, was that those involved in these supposedly hostile breakups, will put on a smile, do the right thing, and be civil to each other on the day, understanding that this day is not about them, and any improper behaviour could ruin the wedding for everyone else.

Yes, I am sure it can be uncomfortable for some people involved, but they are grown adults, and if they love you, they will deal with their issues and make sure it doesn't become a problem on the day. On occasion, I have been told that parents of the bride or groom will not – under any circumstances – appear in the same photo together, only to see them at the wedding happily chatting together like long lost friends. I have even seen signs of romance re-emerging in estranged couples. Mostly, these separated parents are very amicable with each other on the wedding day, especially as there is nothing like the wedding of a son or daughter to remind you of a bond you once shared with the person you now consider an absolute arsehole.

What I would advise is to make sure you tell your photographer beforehand about any complicated relationships or family situations. They should ask you this in advance, but it's best to notify them if they don't, in order to avoid any potentially awkward moments during the group photos.

Having photographed weddings for over a decade, and seen how important photos are to a wedding, this is the part where I am supposed to tell you how your photographer is one of the most important elements of your wedding (although nowhere near as important as the colour scheme, of course), and no expense should be spared when choosing him or her. Except, I don't agree with that at all.

Nowadays more than ever, the role of the wedding photographer has diminished. Photographers now must compete with dozens of guests armed with SLRs, the latest compact camera, or one gazillion megapixel smartphones, all of which are capable of taking very decent photos. And with all these guests snapping away all day, you can (if you want) get thousands of photos for free. And with the way photographic technology is advancing, it's not going to be too long before the consumer gadget in your pocket can rival the quality of a professional-grade camera.

The role of the wedding photographer is, in my experience, more about people management than photography skills anyway. You can be the most talented photographer in the world, with the best equipment money can buy, but if you can't gather together a group of tipsy aunts and uncles, or make a nervous bride or awkward groom feel a little less nervous and awkward, then there is no hope.

When choosing a wedding photographer, it is vitally important to ask to see a finished album or a complete set of photos from one wedding. Any photographer can assemble a portfolio of half-decent photos, without ever actually photographing a wedding, just from snapping a few photos as a wedding guest. I know because that's how I assembled my first portfolio. It is fine to book an inexperienced photographer, but make sure the price reflects it. Photographers' styles vary considerably and by viewing an entire album, you will get a better idea of whether their work is suited to you.

I had one bride and groom who arranged a meeting with me, and they sat and silently flicked through two of my albums, smiling all the while and looking like they were happy with the quality of photos. When they had finished, they closed the albums and the bride said to me, 'There are lots of photos of the guests.' She said it with a big smile, and I interpreted it as a compliment.

'Yes, I like to try and capture lots of natural photos of all your friends and family enjoying your special day.'

'Yeah... I... no,' she said.

'I'm sorry. No what? You don't like that?'

'No, I'm not really interested in lots of photos of all these random people.'

'Well they obviously wouldn't be random people if it was your wedding album. They would be your friends and family. People you have invited to share your wedding.'

'I know. I just don't think I want lots of photos of random people. We'd rather it just be photos of me and Bobby, wouldn't we Bobby?'

'Er... yeah, I guess,' said Bobby.

'Well, as you can see, it's not just photos of 'random people',' I said. I even did the air quotes with my fingers. What a twat. 'There are a lot of photos of the couple too. In fact, the majority of the photos are of the bride and groom. There are about 400 photos in that album, so obviously they won't ALL be of you both.'

She cocked her head and looked at me as if to say, '*why not?*'

I was just about to make my excuses and suggest they find an alternative photographer when she said, 'Well, anyway, we'd like to book you.'

I reluctantly agreed – a job is a job – and I photographed their wedding as I would any other. I toned down the number of photos of 'random people' that I included in their finished album, and they were delighted with the results.

Rachel and I had a friend of a friend photograph our wedding. He had never photographed a wedding before, but he was a keen photographer, with decent equipment, and lots of enthusiasm. He was also very cheap. It was a bit of a gamble, but we didn't have huge expectations for our photography so were happy to take a chance and we were thrilled with his photos. He was still at our wedding enjoying the party when we left at midnight and we have remained friends since.

You need to have a photographer you feel comfortable with. Whether you hire a friend, or a friend of a friend, or some fine-art fancy-pants photographer, insist on meeting them before confirming your booking. If they are a dick and you don't feel comfortable in their company, then don't hire them, however good their photos.

I always feel a huge sense of liberation after the final group shot is ticked off my list. It's the most challenging part of the day for a wedding photographer and it's always a relief when I've got through them all.

The rest of the guests all mingle about, and I suggest to Jen and Matt that we spend a few minutes getting some couple shots of the two of them together while the light is still good. Jen and Matt wander down the driveway, hand in hand, and I snap away from a distance, giving them a few minutes to themselves. This is usually the first time after getting married where it is just the bride and groom on their own together. Even if it's only a couple of minutes, it's important for them to enjoy this brief moment of peace during their day.

I catch up with them at the gate and we spend a few minutes getting some photos on the adjacent country lane, and a couple of other picturesque locations around the venue. Some photographers drag these couple shots out into a full-on photoshoot. And some couples actually request this. I have been a guest at a wedding where the bride and groom have disappeared for their couple shots for an hour and a half. I'm sure their photos were amazing – at least I bloody well hope they were – but to get these photos, they have had to sacrifice a huge chunk of their day. And for what? Will they remember their wedding as a perfect day spent with friends and family, or a day traipsing through fields trying to create the illusion of a perfect wedding?

Ten minutes is plenty of time to get a good selection of romantic photos and allow you to get back to your guests to enjoy the rest of the reception.

'That's it. You're all done,' I say to Jen and Matt. 'You don't have to pose for any more photos today.'

'Great!' says Matt.

'Thanks George. You've been amazing today. I was a bit nervous about having my photo taken, but you've made it seem really easy.'

'It's been my pleasure. Now go and enjoy the rest of your day.'

There is still a lot of the wedding to go. Half an hour of the drinks reception, the meal, the speeches, cutting of the cake, bouquet toss, first dance, but the rest of the day is easy in comparison. I have no more photos to arrange or stage today. I have no more photos to arrange or stage ever.

Back in the courtyard, the drinks are flowing, and a group of young children are picking up bits of confetti from the floor, mixed with gravel, and throwing it at Jen and Matt as they return to talk to their guests. The atmosphere is buzzing, and Jen laughs as Matt pretends he has a piece of gravel stuck in his eye. It turns out he does have a piece of gravel stuck in his eye, but he carries on smiling, and Jen carries on laughing.

Children at weddings can be a contentious issue. Some people believe that children ruin weddings. Yes, children can be bloody annoying and can mistakenly throw gravel instead of confetti, but they also contribute a lot to the fun atmosphere of a wedding.

I would estimate about 90% of the weddings that I photographed had at least some children present. The remaining 10% were undoubtedly the dullest weddings I attended. Sometimes it was a while before I realised there were no children at the wedding. There would be a niggling feeling in my mind that the wedding was missing something, and then I would notice the absence of children's laughter.

Some couples are precious about the thought that children might be noisy during the ceremony. If you want your service to be quiet and noise-free, then get married alone. But, remember that parents will do their best to keep children quiet and well-behaved during the important bits, and if a baby does cry or a child shouts out at an inappropriate time, then all it does is help lighten the atmosphere and diffuse any tension.

I have photographed a few weddings where the bride and groom felt so strongly about their no-children policy at their wedding that they didn't even allow the sons and daughters of their siblings – their own nieces and nephews – to attend. Despite polite protests from the siblings, the bride and groom wouldn't relent, and there was an awkward feeling of resentment throughout these weddings.

Likewise, at the reception, having children running around only adds to the sense of fun. Or better still, get them involved. The honour of being a page boy or flower girl is immense for a child. They don't necessarily have to do anything, and you don't even need to give them a specific role. The title alone is enough to make them feel part of such an important day.

Weddings are hugely important for children. I can clearly remember my aunt and uncle's wedding when I was a child. It felt like a very significant day in my life. It was my first time wearing a suit. My first time handing out confetti. My first time being treated as a grown up. My first time staining a car's paintwork with shaving foam.

My opinion about dogs at weddings is not so liberal.

When I first got into wedding photography, I didn't think pets would figure at all. Soon after I started, I realised that it was quite a popular thing. Pets, specifically dogs, are considered such an important part of the family that they are often included in the wedding plans. Not just included, they are sometimes treated as one of the most important guests.

I have one piece of advice when it comes to including your pets in your wedding.

Don't.

It's an awful idea and you will only live to regret it. Here's why.

There are plenty of things that can and will go wrong. Your dog could jump up with its muddy paws all over your beautiful white dress. I realise I have already told you not to be precious about your wedding dress, but it's one thing to have champagne sloshed on your dress, and another to have a smear of dog shit all down your front for the duration of your special day. Your dog might eat your rings. I know it's unlikely, but if you've foolishly allowed it to be the ringbearer (as many couples inexplicably do), then it's not unheard of. Your dog might get freaked out by all the noise and the people and turn psychotic, biting the hand off an overly-friendly flower girl.

'But', I hear you plead, *'I want our dog to be there to witness such an important part of our life. Surely that's worth the risks?'* No. Trust me, your dog really doesn't care that you are getting married. It doesn't understand the concept of marriage. Because it is a dog.

'But what if our dog just makes a quick appearance to pose for a couple of photos and then is taken away?' Ok, that's fine, if it really means that much to you, and as long as you don't overly hype the significance of these photos, then by all means go for it.

I have photographed several weddings with dogs. In most cases, the dog thankfully just made a brief appearance, the bride and groom gave it some attention, we had some photos, and then a kind friend or neighbour took it away. But a couple of weddings, however, got completely out of hand with the amount of time devoted to their beloved pet.

One couple insisted that their dog, Scruffyshit – or whatever it was called – join them for the romantic couple shots. Not just some of the photos. Every single one. Scruffyshit had already been with them for the whole duration of the ceremony and the bride then insisted on holding him for all the photos of her and her new husband, too. I kept asking the bride if she could put Scruffyshit down. Down on the floor, I mean, not end his life. I'm not that heartless. But she was adamant she was going to hang on to Scruffyshit for all the photos. In every single wedding photograph I took of the bride and groom, it was always the happy couple, and their fucking dog, Scruffyshit.

I understand that your dog is the most important thing in your life right now (apart from your wedding's colour scheme, obviously), but I hate to be the bearer of bad news… it won't always be. Your dog is unlikely to outlive you. When you look back at your photos in decades to come, you might, dare I say it, have had several more dogs by then. Maybe you loved Scruffyshit the Second and Scruffyshit the Third even more than the original Scruffyshit. There is a strong possibility that all that love you once had for your dog later became directed at children that you went on to have together. You will look back at your wedding photos and think, *'oh my god, what the hell was wrong with us? What were we thinking? There we are on our wedding day, the best day of our lives. We look so happy, but who is that big scruffy shit in between us? What was his name again?*

TEN

Professional photographers attract amateur photographers. At nearly every single one of the weddings I photographed, I had at least one guest come up to me and start chatting to me about camera equipment.

'Is that the 70-300mm IS mark one?' he (it was almost always a he) would say.

'Er… I'm not sure. Yes, I think so,' I would say, examining my lens closely for the very first time.

'I've got the mark 2. I just feel like it responds that fraction of a second quicker. And its depth of field when the f-stop is at the lower end is just phenomenal.'

My eyes would glaze over.

'Yeah. I've heard it's phenomenal,' I would say.

'What flash are you using?'

'I don't know,' I would say. 'A 520 or something, maybe?'

'Canon don't make a 520. It will either be a 430 or a 580, unless of course you have the older out-of-date 550.'

'Oh, 580 then I guess.'

'Good choice. Mark I or mark II?'

'I don't know,' I would say, reluctantly retrieving my flash from the bag and seeing that it is a 580ex mark ii. 'It's the mark ii. Do you have the mark iii?'

He would look at me with a look of genuine confusion.

'They don't make a mark iii. At least, not yet. I'll go to the expo later in the year to see what announcements they have.'

'Ok, coooool,'

This type of conversation would pan out like this at almost every wedding. Occasionally, if they were particularly persistent, I would find it tedious, but I mostly found it flattering and humbling. These guys were keen – often obsessive – photographers in their spare time. It was a hobby they were so passionate about that they would happily spend their hard-earned money on owning the very latest of everything. They were desperate to share their knowledge and passion about photography – or camera equipment mostly – to anyone that would want to hear. And surely who would want to talk about cameras more than a professional photographer? Unfortunately, my knowledge of the latest camera equipment and technicalities of my kit was rather limited. But I was once like them too. Well, I was never obsessed enough, nor wealthy enough, to afford the latest or best equipment. But when I was starting out in photography, before it became a job, I would spend hours a day on photography forums and in camera shops, learning about photography and geeking out about the latest technology.

When I first started shadowing a local photographer to gain some valuable work experience, I asked him questions about his camera equipment while we sat in the car together on the way to jobs. Two things surprised me. Firstly, he didn't seem to know as much as I did about the latest camera equipment. And secondly, and extremely confusingly for me at the time, he didn't seem to care.

It wasn't until I became a professional photographer that I realised how little importance I gave to my equipment. Once I had a decent set of lenses and a couple of adequate camera bodies, I spent no more time in camera shops or on the forums. I didn't have the time or inclination to spend what little free time I had talking about cameras, and I certainly didn't want to spend all the money I was earning from photography on newer camera equipment.

But I remembered what I had been like before photography was my career, and always did my best to sound enthusiastic and welcoming to camera geeks. And, more than that, when people started talking to me so enthusiastically about cameras and photography, it made me realise how incredibly fortunate I was to be paid to do something that millions of people pursue as a hobby.

I confess that my technical knowledge of photography is and always has been a bit limited. I never understood the functions on my camera as well as perhaps I should have. I genuinely had no idea what many of the buttons did, nor how to utilise lots of the settings. But I could take a decent picture and I was a damn good wedding photographer. The technical side of it I was able to blag. Dare I say it, and perhaps it's foolish to write it here, but it's similar to my career as an author. Technically, I am pretty crap. I really shouldn't be trusted with a computer. I don't know what a fronted adverbial is, I don't know what a subordinate clause is, I don't know what a relative pronoun is. These are all things a writer should probably know. I confess, I don't. But I can just about string a sentence together. And if you string enough sentences together, one after another, then eventually you have a book.

Where was I, before I started confessing to be a crap writer? Ah yes, I was talking about photography enthusiasts at weddings.

As well as the photo nerds, there were always several other keen photographers at weddings, armed with professional-grade SLRs and often with a better selection of lenses than my own. These photographers always observed me from a distance, with a slight look of superiority that implied they should be the ones taking the photos, and not me. I have heard of other professional

135

wedding photographers taking a stand against these wannabes, almost viewing them as a threat. I have been a guest at weddings where the professional photographer has taken the bridal party away to do the formal photos and told other guests they are not allowed to follow them to photograph the group shots.

These same professional photographers also make their physical presence as prominent as possible during key moments like the cutting of the cake and the first dance, attempting to form a human shield so that others can't get the same photo.

If a professional photographer feels threatened by the presence of other photographers, then perhaps they shouldn't be in the business. Of course these other photographers will get some good photos. Why shouldn't they? They have every right to be able to take photos at the wedding. We are the lucky ones, remember. We are getting paid, they are not.

I always encouraged guests to get the best angles for their photos too. During the cutting of the cake or signing of the register, I would quickly take my photos and then duck out of the way and beckon others forwards to take theirs.

During the big group shot when I would often be perched at the top of a stepladder, sometimes a guest or family member – usually an elderly grandma, with nerves of steel – would step forward with her little compact camera and ask me if I could take one with her camera too. I would happily oblige, which would result in several other guests rushing forwards with their cameras or phones too. I would then be perched precariously on this step ladder juggling an armful of different cameras and phones. I quite enjoyed it and I hope it helped the guests warm to me a little bit more.

There is still about half an hour until the guests will be called in to the start of Jen and Matt's wedding breakfast. The 'wedding breakfast' is a predominantly British phrase and is confusing as it is not a breakfast in either its menu or timing. In pre-reformation weddings, the couple marrying would fast the previous night, and their wedding meal would be breaking their fast. It is also the first meal that the bride and groom will have together as a married couple, so the term 'breakfast' has tenuously stuck around.

I slip into the room where they will be eating their wedding breakfast to take some photos of the décor and table decorations before the guests are called through. It's a spectacular converted barn with candelabras hanging from the ceiling. It's beginning to get dark outside and the room feels cosy and atmospheric, with flickering candles on every table and warm autumnal floral arrangements.

Flowers have a close association with weddings. If you picture a bride standing outside a church, the image you form in your mind will almost always have her clutching a bouquet of flowers. It seems so natural and fitting that the bride would carry flowers. Flowers are beautiful, the bride is beautiful, they are the perfect accessory to each other.

It wasn't always this way, however. As far back as the middle ages, evidence exists of the bride carrying a bouquet. But it was not a bouquet of flowers, but of garlic and strong-smelling herbs like dill and chives. This pungent arrangement served many purposes: it was said to scare away evil spirits (and presumably any men who fancied their chances), it provided a distraction to the smell of death and served as a healing antidote during times of plague, and it was also – in times when hygiene and sanitation were not the concern they are today – used to mask the body odour of the bride. Next time you see a bride with a bouquet, remember the rule… the bigger her bouquet, the more pungent her BO.

Over time, this herbal arrangement was replaced with flowers, and these bouquets have become more elaborate and expensive over the years, to the extent you often see the bride hauling around what appears to be an exhibit from the Chelsea Flower Show.

I photographed Jen and her bridesmaids' bouquets this morning right after they were delivered to the house and were looking their best. They were elegant and simple – an understated, but perfectly chosen bunch of seasonal autumnal flowers, tied together with brown string.

If you are going to have a bouquet, which you probably will as it gives you something to do with your hands (unless of course you get a wedding dress with pockets – it could be the next big thing), please don't be overly protective of it. It is just a bunch of flowers. An accessory. Get something that is simple, sturdy and can cope with being knocked, dropped and bashed around a bit. And don't get something so heavy that you need one of your bridesmaids to help you carry it.

Table centrepieces have become more and more elaborate over the years, getting bigger and bigger and more and more ridiculous. Flowers on tables do help brighten up the room, but, again, keep them simple. The guests will be far more interested in chatting to each other, eating, drinking and looking at you, than caring at all about the table centrepieces. Make sure they don't block people's line of sight. I have photographed so many weddings where the guests have been unable to see each other because of the huge shrubberies growing from the centre of the table. I have been at receptions that have felt more like I was in a subtropical biosphere than a wedding.

If you happen to have a lot of bridesmaids, leave empty vases on the tables and ask the bridesmaids to put their bouquets into the vases during the meal. They will more than make do as a table centrepiece and the bridesmaids will be delighted to be rid of their bouquets for a while.

I photograph the candles and the table centrepieces and look around at the other table decorations. It was all going so well with Jen and Matt's wedding. Up until now they had done everything right. Then I see that they have opted for disposable cameras on their tables. I roll my eyes out loud.

Disposable cameras have been popular at weddings for as long as there have been disposable cameras. They are left on the tables during the wedding breakfast for guests to take photos of whatever they like, and for the bride and groom to develop later to see what imaginative and creative shots have been taken. Back in the day, before most guests had digital cameras or smartphones, this might have been an acceptable idea. Nowadays, it is nonsensical. Save yourself the unnecessary expense and disappointment and avoid disposable cameras.

First of all, most guests, especially when they are drunk, don't know how to use a disposable camera. Despite being the most basic type of technological equipment around, with usually only a couple of buttons at most, people will still get it wrong. The cameras tend to get used mostly indoors, and the majority of the guests will forget to press the flash button, so you will be left with a series of shitty dark silhouetted images. Secondly, disposable cameras don't have autofocus (or even manual focus, for that matter) so the focus is very unlikely to be sharp. Lastly, after a few drinks, people will want to use these cameras to take all sorts of ridiculous photos. And unlike in the digital era, there is no delete button on a disposable camera. I've seen drunken guests taking photos of breasts, bare arses, guests vomiting and even a group of lads emerging from the toilets boasting about how the bride and groom can play a *guess whose dick pic?* game when they get back from their honeymoon. What a treat that would be for them.

You will have a brief moment of excitement and anticipation as you wait for the photo lab to develop your photos, but this feeling will be very short lived when you flick through and discover that 50% of your photos are so dark that it is indistinguishable who is in them, 25% are so out of focus it is indistinguishable who is in them, and in the other 25% it is indistinguishable whose dick is whose.

I know that people abuse disposable cameras at weddings because I have been one of those people. Not for dick pics, I should add. Rachel and I were guests at the wedding of one of her university friends. We had a disposable camera on our table and I used up every single one of the 24 exposures taking close-ups of the people sat either side of me every time they stuffed a fork-full of food into their mouth. It kept me amused for the whole meal (I was pretty drunk, I confess), and if we hadn't been at a wedding, I think Rachel would have divorced me.

When the couple returned from honeymoon and got all their disposable cameras developed, the bride and groom said how our set of photos was by far the best out of everyone's. This should not be taken as a compliment about my photography skills. It just illustrates how shit the other photos must have been.

By all means set up a shared online folder and encourage guests to upload their photos, but forget the disposable camera. It's had its day. But, if underexposed, out of focus dick pics are your thing, hey, get stocked up.

I forgive Jen and Matt for the disposable camera faux pas – they are not to know what shitty photos await them. The rest of the room looks stunning and I enjoy these few minutes of peace and quiet, roaming the room, photographing all the little details.

140

There has been a common theme throughout this book. I have highlighted a lot of aspects of weddings that are totally unnecessary and a complete waste of time and money. The favours – the small gifts usually left on the table for guests as a way of saying thank you for being a part of the wedding – fit the bill of being totally unnecessary and a complete waste of time and money perhaps more than any other element of the wedding.

But, do you know what? I bloody love favours! I am not a materialistic person in the slightest. I hate accumulating crap, and would much rather give gifts than receive them. But no matter how small or simple, I am a big fan of favours. As a guest, it doesn't matter if it's a low-key or elaborate wedding, never mind whether it's a fun and energetic wedding or a slow and tedious one, if I find a small packet of sweets next to my name place, my day is made.

The tradition of favours is said to have been started by European aristocracy. Small, ornate trinket boxes made from precious stones were filled with sugar cubes and given to guests as a present during special occasions. When sugar became more readily available, and therefore 'common', aristocrats used almonds instead. Five almonds were used to symbolise health, wealth, happiness, fertility and long life. For centuries, sugared almonds were the standard favour until more modern times when brides and grooms became more adventurous.

Favours can provide an opportunity for a bride and groom to get creative. But only if they want to. It doesn't take much to please me. I would be happy with some sugared almonds.

Lottery scratch cards have become popular as wedding favours. I don't know why, as 90% of the guests will be big losers. The very few who do win are often then encouraged to buy a round of drinks or donate the money to the bride and groom. So, either way, all the guests go home empty-handed.

I have seen some brilliant wedding favours over the years, including bottles of home-brewed beer, sloe gin, chilli sauce, homemade chocolates, seeds, and CD mixtapes of the bride and groom's favourite songs. All of these are relatively low cost and your guests will have a lasting memory of your wedding that will outlive the disappointment of a losing lottery ticket.

Charity donations are another common one. *We have made a donation to* [insert charity name here] *in lieu of buying wedding favours.'* Fuck that shit! Don't do this. It comes across as very sanctimonious. Wedding favours, if done simply, don't have to cost much money. They don't have to cost anything at all. Making a donation to charity makes the favours all about you again. The favours are a chance to show that your wedding is not all about you. If you want to make a donation to charity, that's fantastic, good for you, but you don't need to brag about it to everyone at your wedding. Often the same people who have donated to charity in lieu of favours will have happily wasted several hundred pounds on pointless accessories, such as a fancy cake knife that they will use only once. Make that donation to charity. But make it privately, and give your guests some sugared almonds, you stingy bastards.

For our wedding favours, Rachel and I gave our guests a small cardboard box full of sweets and a personalised pebble. We had a vague seaside theme, which was a little weird when we got married in the Midlands. I'm not sure that we even had a colour scheme for our wedding, or if we did, I wasn't consulted on it. Each pebble had the guest's name written on it in a fancy paint. I tried helping but was fired after one pebble, as my writing was deemed too scruffy. These pebbles acted as the name place holder, but almost all of them were taken home by the guests. Many of our friends still have their pebbles, cluttering up mantelpieces or bookshelves around the world, but it's a useful reminder for them, in case they ever forget their own name.

Jen and Matt have made personalised chocolates for their favours. Each guest has been given a round, flat chocolate – about the size of the base of a wine glass – with Jen and Matt's names and the date of the wedding written in white chocolate. They look very nice – a little pointless, but that's the beauty of favours – and they will be well received. Most guests will just eat theirs, some as soon as they sit down, some before they sit down, but others will take theirs home for a memento of the wedding and leave them to fester in a drawer somewhere, before finding it many years later and wishing they had just eaten it at the wedding. I take a photo of one for the album.

Over by the door, I photograph Jen and Matt's Table Plan.

The table plan causes weeks of headaches for many couples. Brides and grooms stress and argue about who sits next to whom, and which tables should be adjacent to which. People won't care about where they sit nearly as much as you think they will. Sit couples together, so that people will at least know another person on their table, and then don't worry too much about where everyone else goes.

Or dispense with the table plan completely. I have photographed and been a guest at several weddings without any sort of table plan. And this worked seamlessly. People just filled up places wherever. Some moved places between courses, but nobody lost their shit, so don't lose yours by over-thinking it.

Apart from the disposable cameras, Jen and Matt have got the balance of their room just about perfect. When sorting out the little details for your wedding, the temptation is to go for everything that takes your fancy. Every different table decoration, wall hanging, or ornament that you see you will want to find a place for somewhere in the room. It's a common mistake to fill your venue with far too much crap. I've walked into some venues and had a genuine claustrophobic panic attack as though I was trapped in some horrendous Aladdin's cave hell. If you overdo it with the décor, it becomes far too distracting. If you confuse your guests with too much to look at, they will end up seeing none of it.

ELEVEN

James, the best man, enters the room. He's holding a big armful of cards and a couple of presents.

'Hi George. Wow, it looks awesome in here.'

'Yes, they've done a great job. How's it all going out there?'

'Good. Everyone seems to be enjoying themselves. Any idea where these are supposed to go?' His eyes dart to the armful of cards and presents he's carrying. 'I seem to have been demoted from best man to postman.'

'There's a present table over there in the corner by the cake.'

The present table already has a scattering of cards and a couple of what look like bottles of wine – either that or cleverly wrapped Toblerones. I noticed on Jen and Matt's wedding invitation, when I photographed it earlier this morning, that they had set up a honeymoon fund in lieu of presents, but that never stops a few guests who insist on bringing a gift on the day.

Wedding gifts have been present for as long as documentation of weddings exist. A dowry used to be paid to the happy couple in the form of land or animals. This is so much better than modern day wedding lists. It would be nice if this ancient custom made a comeback. Instead of that set of microwavable casserole dishes, Auntie Susie gives you a corner of her garden. And instead of that shiny new toaster, cousin Neil gives you a small donkey. I think it's a fantastic idea.

The first recorded example of a store wedding list was at Marshall Field's (now Macy's) in Chicago. Other stores soon followed suit and wedding lists grew into the big multi-million-dollar industry they are today. Wedding lists are a difficult dilemma. It's impossible to write a list of presents that you want without coming across as a couple of spoiled dickheads. Also, with potentially over a hundred guests to cater for, all with different budgets, you will most likely find yourself adding lots of completely unnecessary items to your list just for the sake of it. It creates all sorts of uncomfortable situations while a couple browse a department store to compile their gift list.

'Oh, look Maria, they've got the same teapot we have, but in purple.'

'I don't think we need another teapot, Steve. We don't even use the green one we already have.'

'Well we need some more items in the cheaper price range. And maybe we would use the teapot more if it was purple?'

'Fine, add it to the list then.'

There is something ugly and materialistic about a department store wedding list. The need to think of things that we want, just to give our guests something to buy for us, to stop them feeling guilty about not giving us a gift, seems inherently wrong. But, on the other hand, if you don't have a list, you will just end up with a ton of crap you don't need or even want.

Another popular option – as Jen and Matt have opted for – is to have a honeymoon fund that people can contribute to, to help pay for travels together as a couple. Rachel and I did this too, and the generosity of our guests allowed us to book flights to South America the year after we married. If this still feels too impersonal, there are companies that provide wedding lists that allow guests to pay for particular experiences on a honeymoon. For example, you could pay for a couple to go snorkelling, or hire bikes, or go to the theatre, or spend the night in a posh hotel. This way, you have a specific connection to their honeymoon and when they are enjoying that moment on their trip, they can remember the person who bought it. While relishing some honeymoon fun-time in a lavish hotel booked via the wedding list, the bride or groom can lie back in their bed and whisper, 'thank you, Grandma.' On second thoughts, perhaps not. Maybe just ask for land or animals instead.

If the idea of any form of gift list repulses you, how about requesting donations to a charity that you would like to support? Unlike donating to charity in lieu of favours, this IS an acceptable idea, and I very much encourage it. Just so long as I still get my sugared almonds.

Jen and Matt's guests will be called into the room in the next few minutes, so I finish my photos in the barn and head for the door to get a few final shots in the last moments of daylight. Everyone is in high-spirits out in the courtyard, and I snap away while they continue to sip their drinks. Unlike that self-centred bride and groom I mentioned earlier, Jen and Matt are keen to have photos of these 'random people' and I need lots of candid photos to use in their wedding album.

As part of most of the weddings I photographed, I provided a large hardback photobook included in the package. The album usually ran to at least 120 pages and contained over 400 photos. It was an effective way to present a lot of photos, documenting the entire day, without the cost and impracticality of a traditional album. Rather than go through the design process of the album with the bride and groom, asking them to select their preferred photos and choose the layout, I would assemble the first draft, based on my experience of what works in a photo album. I would then send them a digital version of the album, usually while the couple were still on their honeymoon, for them to look through. This would allow them to request any changes to the album before it was printed, and it was also an effective way for them to see all their photos presented as a story so they could relive their special day.

Many couples would look through the album and ask me to order it exactly as it was. I would like to claim that this was because I was so finely tuned into the wants and needs of the couple that I could design the album to their exact specifications without liaising with them. But it was usually down to laziness on the part of the bride and groom. This laziness suited me perfectly. I could take one last flick through the digital version to check for any problems, then click 'order' and have the book delivered directly to the couple and my work with them was done.

Usually, the couple would request a handful of changes. Perhaps a more flattering angle for one of the bridal portraits, or the removal of a photo of Uncle Nigel's girlfriend who was no longer his girlfriend, and who they never really liked anyway. These changes took very little time and I was happy they had made the effort to check that the book was exactly as they wanted.

I would sometimes get an email asking me to make 'a few' amendments, and I would scroll down to see a list detailing that almost every photo and every page layout was now being altered to something else. This was time-consuming for me, but again I was happy that at least the finished product would be to their liking.

One particular occasion stands out. I was sent a list of amendments as soon as a couple returned from their honeymoon. I was impressed with how prompt they had been – some couples took years, and some still haven't got back to me. The bride had thanked me for the lovely photos and asked if I could make a few amendments which she had detailed. She listed about twenty photos and asked for each to be replaced with twenty different photos which she had also listed. It wasn't until I started making the changes that I realised there was something unusual about her request.

The first photo on the list was a strong black and white picture of the groom and best man strolling casually down the church path. I thought it was a fantastic image, but I understand that people's tastes vary. However, she had swapped it for a photo of the order of service. It wasn't a particularly remarkable photo, and it certainly wasn't the most photogenic order of service I have ever seen. As previously mentioned, I would take photos of all the little details of the day, but apart from the photos of the rings and bouquets, these would usually be used on montage pages to illustrate the different elements that the couple had spent months or years obsessing over. Still, if the bride wanted to swap a classic pre-wedding photo of the groom and best man for a photo of the order of service – which was, incidentally, already included on another page – then that was absolutely fine by me.

Her next amendment involved swapping a photo of the best man handing over the rings in the church. Again, who am I to question someone's taste in photos? The photo she had swapped it for was a wide-angle photo of the outside of the church. A picture, almost identical, but not as nice, as one I had included a few pages previously. I continued through the list, each time surprised that a decent photo had been swapped for an inferior one. It was after about half a dozen photos that I realised there was a common theme connecting all of these photos. She wasn't asking for them to be removed because she didn't like the photo. She was asking for them to be removed because of who was in them. Every single one of her amendments so far contained the same person. Every single one was a photo of the best man.

My heart started racing. Was it just these particular photos of him she didn't like? I worked my way through the rest of her list and then had a flick through the entire book, and noticed to my horror that, apart from a couple of big group shots and wide-angle shots of the venue, every photo featuring the best man had been removed. It was as if he wasn't even at the wedding.

The couple had only returned from their honeymoon the day before she emailed me. What the hell had happened between me leaving the wedding and them contacting me? I worried for a moment that perhaps the best man had recently died, but then realised you would be pretty heartless to remove all trace of him if that was the case. If anything, you would want to honour his memory. I then wondered if perhaps the best man and groom had had a big fallout, and that he had requested the removal of all the photos. This was possible, but they seemed very close, and blokes are usually pretty good at getting over arguments quickly. There was something about it that made me fairly certain that it was the bride who had some sort of issue with the best man. The groom looked happy in all his photos with the best man. But any photos involving the best man and the bride – the handing over of the rings, the best man's speech – the bride did not look so happy. She wore an expression that suggested she had an issue with the best man. But was it an issue? Or was it, perhaps, history? I flicked through the photos again and couldn't work it out. If the bride and best man had history, then the groom was looking remarkably ok with it. In fact, he and the best man looked very happy indeed. Perhaps too happy. Maybe the groom didn't know about this infidelity. Or maybe the groom and best man were the ones who had history and the bride had only recently found out about it? Or maybe the bride and best man got together later that night? It was all so scandalous and I was desperate to know the answer. I made all the changes and emailed the bride to tell her it was all done.

At the end of the message, I added the line, '*I couldn't help noticing that all of the photos you removed were of the best man. Do you mind me asking the reason for this?*' I was about to click *send* but then wimped out. I deleted the line as it seemed unprofessional. I then ordered the album, and I am still no wiser about the mystery. Perhaps I'll invent my own conclusion to the story, and you'll be able to read all about it in my sexy romance thriller – *Beauty and the Best Man* - out next year.

TWELVE

The art of altering photos is not a by-product of the Instagram generation. Even film photographers could and did use many tricks to manipulate photos after they had been taken. Technology has advanced so much in recent years that it is so easy to change photos, make people more attractive, give images more spark and basically make average photos better.

I very rarely did any post-production with my photos, other than a batch conversion to black and white. This was partly because I like photographs in their natural state, but also because I knew if I embarked on a quest to make every image perfect, I would never leave my computer.

With all the possibilities that modern technology offers us, I understand that we should embrace it and allow wedding photographers to express their creativity at their computers as well as when behind the camera. Increasing the dynamic range of the sky in a dramatic couple shot, or boosting the contrast and saturation of colours to make for a more impressive sunset is definitely justifiable. As is removing an unsightly traffic cone from a photo, or an errant dog turd outside the church door. What is not acceptable, in my opinion, is manipulating photos so excessively that the finished images bear no relation to the actual day.

If each and every photo is heavily airbrushed so that your skin is flawless and your eyes unnaturally big, you will either look back at your wedding remembering that a lot of post-production went in to making you look that good, or you will end up hating your future self, because of the misguided belief that you will never look as good as you did on your wedding day.

Emma was one of the most fun brides I ever photographed. She was loud, confident and hilarious. She was also curvy. She looked great, and I knew she would be an easy bride to photograph; a radiant smile being far more beautiful to a camera lens than a slim figure. We had our pre-wedding meeting in a coffee shop, and our coffees were served with a shot glass of M&M's. Emma told me she was concerned about her weight and I told her – truthfully – that I thought she looked fantastic. She then confessed that her dad had offered to pay her a financial reward if she was able to shed a few pounds before her wedding. This seemed like a horrendous way to knock her self-confidence, and her quiet and obedient fiancé Martin said all the right things to try and dissuade her from worrying about her weight. Emma said she wasn't going to eat her M&Ms, so Martin and I resisted eating ours too.

At the end of the meeting, we walked towards the exit to say goodbye. I pulled open the door to let them out of the café, when I noticed Emma was no longer with us. I turned to see her back at our table, where she picked up all three shot glasses of M&Ms, and knocked back the contents of each, one after the other. She jogged back to us smiling, without any chocolate in her mouth, having seemingly swallowed the lot without chewing. 'Don't tell Dad', she whispered to Martin.

'Are you going to be able to photoshop my wedding photos to make me look slimmer?' Emma said outside.

I laughed, assuming that she was joking, and told her I wouldn't be doing any photoshopping and that she would look fabulous as she was.

The wedding day was a great success and Emma was in fine form, bright and smiley throughout the day. I was really pleased with my photos and put together a beautiful album for them both. A couple of weeks after Emma and Martin returned from honeymoon, I received a CD in the post and a letter with a list of amendments I was to make to the photobook. Rather than the usual swapping photos for other photos, this list almost exclusively asked me to change specific photos with edited versions on the CD.

I tentatively opened the photos on the CD one by one. The changes were immediately obvious. It seemed that when Emma had asked if I could photoshop her thinner, she hadn't been joking. And with my refusal to do so, the job had been passed on to her obedient husband Martin. In each of the photos, all of which were side profile shots of the bride, her neck, which had once curved smoothly down towards her chest, had now dramatically disappeared leaving a sharp and angular face. Her chin had been photoshopped away so much that some of her jaw was also missing. Where she once had nice, smooth rounded features, she now had the profile of Tutankhamun with his beard.

And then my eyes dropped to her arm and I gasped. There were a series of photos of the newly married couple, Emma with her hand on Martin's shoulder, both looking delightfully happy and in love. Only Emma should not have looked so happy, as she appeared to have a huge chunk of her upper arm missing. Once perfectly in proportion with the rest of her body, Emma's bicep now had a large slice taken out of it from the top and bottom.

I stared at the photos in disbelief. I felt a huge amount of sadness for Emma. Nobody else would have looked at the original photos and seen anything other than two happy and beautiful people. All Emma could focus on was her chin and bicep. In the future, when she looked back at her photos, she would surely just remember how Martin had photoshopped her body to make her appear slimmer.

I sent Martin an email thanking him for the CD and politely asking if he was sure he wanted me to make the changes. He replied and said that he agreed with me 100% and much preferred the original photos, but that Emma had insisted that he amend them, and he didn't want to argue with his new wife.

I had no choice but to honour his request. I am no expert at photo editing, but I was a Jedi compared to the botch-job Martin had done. The amateur way that he had digitally hacked at his wife's chin and arm made it immediately obvious that Emma had had more than a bit of work done. If I was going to allow the edited versions of the photos to be included in the finished album, then I could at least make them look as natural as possible. So, I found myself sitting at my desk until the early hours of the morning, digitally smoothing out the pixels of Emma's new chin and bicep so that it blended a little more naturally into the rest of her body and the background. Emma was delighted with the finished album and her new sleek figure.

Rachel wanted a more traditional wedding album for our wedding photos. You know the type, with bits of annoying tracing paper over each page. We made two of them as we had so many photos – one for the day and one for the evening reception. We've hardly ever looked at either. They live in their boxes gathering dust in the back of a cupboard somewhere.

For our tenth wedding anniversary, I put together one of these photobooks (like the ones I made for my wedding couples) for our wedding instead, thinking it was a more practical and convenient way of displaying our photos. That now sits in the cupboard gathering dust too.

This goes to show that you shouldn't worry too much about your photos. You won't look at them nearly as often as you think you will, and nobody else will want to either.

While we are on the subject of digital enhancements, now seems like an appropriate time to discuss filters. As I said, I am a big believer in photos looking as natural as possible. Yes, it's nice to view heavily filtered photos on social media, but when it comes to weddings, in years to come you don't want to look back at your wedding photos as though you got married in high definition. And please don't get me started on people wanting to have their photos converted to sepia.

'Mummy, did you and Daddy get married in the Victorian times?'

'No dear, we just had our photos converted to sepia because they look really good.'

'Do they, Mummy? They look a bit… er… a bit stupid and old-fashioned.'

'Well we know that now, darling, but at the time we thought they looked really good.'

Don't, under any circumstances, have your photos converted to sepia.

Black and white, however, is more than acceptable. I know it's hypocritical, but I feel black and white photos have gained an exemption from ever being considered naff. Black and white photos display a timeless quality that will always appeal.

My hatred of sepia photos is nothing to how I feel about another popular style of photo-manipulation – the colour drop. A colour drop image is a black and white photo, where one element of the image – possibly a bouquet of flowers, a dress, or a shoe – is displayed in colour. I have never, ever, seen a single one of these colour drop images that I like. Every time I see one,

I silently weep and a little piece of me dies inside. Colour drop doesn't make any sense to me. It's like, '*wow, look what we can do with modern technology. We've created this beautiful black and white image and now we can completely fuck it up with a pointless splash of colour.*' Thankfully, it's a style that seems to be on the wane. Hallelujah!

It won't surprise you to hear that Sugar Sweet Precious Memories were big fans of colour drop. On their company website, the main photo on their homepage was a black and white photo of a young bridesmaid, aged about six, with her head turned away from the camera. The young girl was idly holding a bottle of beer, which was the only part of the image in colour, its bright green bottle and vibrant red logo being the most visible part of the website's homepage. It was a terrible choice of image. It's a photo that would not have even made the final edit had I taken it, but such was the photographer's love of colour drop and the fact that a child was HOLDING A BOTTLE OF BEER (SHOCK HORROR) made it somehow justify being the standout photo for the business.

Somehow, Sugar Sweet Precious Memories managed to gather a lot of bookings. This also meant that the majority of those who booked their wedding photography through the business were attracted by the lure of this photo. And that worryingly meant that colour drop was the sort of photo that they wanted.

Thankfully, I was only paid to take the photos. A CD of the files was then passed on to Clive (the business owner) who was then responsible for ruining all of my decent photos with fancy filters and pointless colour drops before putting them together into a disgusting album.

I was forced to shadow Clive for a wedding before he allowed me to photograph my own Sugar Sweet Precious Memories' wedding. I watched as he meticulously worked his way through the strict 108 shot list, ticking each one off as it was done, with absolutely no extra spontaneity or creativity. The final shot on the list after the 'FUN' section said 'OTHER', which was the only shot that allowed the photographer any freedom to stray from this list. Clive said, 'usually best to take a photo of a bridesmaid or a pageboy,' so as we left the building – without saying goodbye to the bride and groom – he paused for half a second and pointed his camera at a young flower girl who was standing idly in a dark corner of the hotel function room. She looked up at him startled. He didn't wait for a smile or try to encourage one. He just took one photo – the final tick on his list, and walked straight out the door. She wasn't even holding a bottle of beer.

THIRTEEN

Jen and Matt look completely relaxed and happy. They couldn't have hoped for better weather for a mid-October wedding. As the sun begins to set, it is getting a little too cold for some of the guests who have moved into the adjacent barn, but most of their friends and family are still outside, standing in the courtyard or sitting on the benches dotted around the venue.

The wedding organiser comes over to check with Jen and Matt that they are happy to be called through to the main barn for their wedding breakfast. An attentive usher – Rob, Matt's brother – appears as if by magic to ask if they would like him to announce people through. He taps his glass with a knife, makes a quick announcement, and the hungry guests begin to shuffle towards the door. Jen and Matt hang back to allow everyone to be seated before their entrance. They have thankfully chosen not to have a receiving line.

The receiving line is an opportunity for the bride and groom and both sets of parents to meet every single one of the guests and thank them for coming to the wedding. It is also a giant ball-ache for everyone at the wedding.

Traditionally, whatever that means, the receiving line consists of the bride and groom, both sets of parents, the best man and the chief bridesmaid (your favourite one), but it can also include basically whoever you like.

I understand the point of the receiving line, and it does make sense as a way to ensure that you have at least said *hello* to every guest. But receiving lines are incredibly tedious and it is not the best use of time at your wedding. Receiving lines always overrun, they make guests bored out of their minds; those at the back of the queue will be so ready for a drink by the time they say *hello*, they will resent you for making them stand in line so long, and those at the front of the queue and first to their seats will be so shitfaced by the time everyone is seated there will be no wine left for anyone else. Your feet will ache, Auntie Maureen will have held up proceedings by spending 15 minutes telling you all about her neighbour Ernie's irritable bowel syndrome, and you will wish you had not bothered with the whole charade. Don't put yourself through it.

You will have spoken to many of your guests already during the reception, and any that you have missed you can catch up with between courses of the meal or during the evening reception. I photographed one wedding where the receiving line shenanigans lasted an hour and a bloody half.

If you choose to ignore my advice and decide to have a receiving line, then make sure you at least tell the caterers in advance. If you have told them you will be sitting down to eat at 4 p.m., they will have prepared the food accordingly. If you then decide to begin an impromptu receiving line, proceedings will be delayed by at least half an hour and your meal will be cold.

I was best man at a wedding where the bride and groom did just that. The husband of the couple running the catering – a particularly scary pair who you wouldn't want to mess with – grabbed me by the arm.

'There was NO mention of a receiving line,' he barked. 'This is why we have TWO pre-wedding meetings to go through every single detail with the bride and groom. This is NOT acceptable. You have to sort this out NOW.'

I had to politely interrupt the bride and groom and tell them that perhaps they should abandon the receiving line they had already started. They did so gladly and there was a look of relief on the faces of the guests in the queue that they didn't have to go through the motions.

If you are a wedding guest stuck at the back of the receiving line, then I've got a top tip for you... fuck it! Instead of wasting your life standing in line, walk purposefully into the room, with a look on your face as though you are just taking something to another guest, and you'll be right back. Go straight past the bride and groom – who will be too busy feigning interest in Auntie Maureen's ramblings to notice you – then take your seat at your table and don't look back. You will have saved yourself at least half an hour of tedium, and gained half an hour of drinking time. The bride and groom won't even have noticed. Make a point of saying *hello* to them on the dancefloor later.

The guests all take their seats and Jen and Matt make their entrance. Everyone stands, whoops and cheers to welcome them in, and then Matt's brother with his loud voice tells everyone they can sit back down. I walk around the room taking some candid photos of the guests sitting at their tables. Nobody looks good when photographed mid-mouthful – unless you are trying to sabotage a disposable camera – so these minutes before the food arrives are very important for me to get some nice relaxed shots of these 'random people' enjoying the day.

After the first course arrives, I move through into the empty bar next door, and take a seat for the first time since early this morning (unless you count the ten-minute car journey). It's a chance for me to sit back and relax. Sometimes I will have a quick flick through the photos of the day so far, but usually I will put my camera down and try and distance myself from the wedding for a few minutes.

On this occasion, I am joined by a videographer. Jayden is in his thirties, very friendly and has been a pleasure to work with.

By that I mean we have hardly even noticed each other, and neither of us have got in each other's way. Reverend David didn't allow filming during the ceremony, so Jayden has only been hired to document the reception.

As professional wedding photography seems to be an industry on the wane, videography has very much increased in popularity. It has developed in style from a more old-fashioned, camera on a tripod, static recording of the day, to a glossy and artistic cinematic movie, with slow-motion segments, powerful music, special effects, and impressive drone footage.

I am undecided about videography at weddings. I have seen lots of finished videos of people's weddings and some of them are seriously beautiful and spectacular. To watch once. Even if I had one of my own wedding, I doubt I would watch it more than a couple of times, and other people certainly wouldn't want to watch it.

Rachel and I had bits of our wedding filmed by her uncle. We watched it when we got back from honeymoon and it was fun to briefly reminisce about our wedding. In 2013, before we moved down to Devon, we did a car-boot sale to try and get rid of a lot of our old stuff. One item we sold was our old VHS player which we never used. After taking the man's £2.50, I had a quick check to make sure we hadn't left a tape inside. Sure enough, I could see the words '*George and Rachel wedding video.*' We had no means of ejecting the tape, so I refunded the £2.50 and we kept the VHS player. Six years later and it is still sitting inside that VHS player in the loft.

If you have the budget and desire to capture your wedding on film, by all means go for it. Just make sure your wedding doesn't become one big movie set. Most videographers – like Jayden at Jen and Matt's wedding – are very discreet and can get great results without interfering with the day at all. Others are less so.

Rachel and I were guests at a wedding where they hired a videographer who brought along a sound technician with a huge boom microphone, and a lighting guy with a full lighting rig, complete with giant strobes. During the church ceremony, they positioned themselves in the aisle, directly in front of the bride and groom. Nobody in the church could even see the happy couple during the service. I have no idea what the finished video looked like. I doubt the couple have either. It's probably sitting in their loft somewhere gathering dust.

A meal arrives for Jayden and me. It's a huge plate of roast beef with all the trimmings – the same meal being served to the guests next-door. Lots of wedding photographers stipulate in their contract that they must be fed. I have listened to angry rants from fellow wedding photographers who berate any couple who would dare to consider not feeding them. *'I am on my feet for 12 hours, goddammit. I need to be fed!'*

Er... yeah... then bring a packed lunch, you moron. What about people in other jobs? Can you imagine a nurse or a firefighter ranting that they didn't get fed during their long shift? As if wedding photography is some superior job that warrants special treatment. I never once asked to be fed at a wedding. Having said that, I also never refused food either. I'm not an idiot.

In most cases, the bride and groom would tell me at our pre-wedding meeting that they were going to arrange food for me. If they didn't, the caterer would often bring me food anyway. If they didn't, then I would grab a packet of crisps from my car, or sometimes just go hungry. What I wouldn't do is start spouting off to anyone that would listen about what a pair of twats the bride and groom were for not giving me a meal. It's their wedding day! They have got more important shit to think about than feeding the photographer. Like their colour scheme.

'Have you ever caught any really embarrassing moments on film?' I ask Jayden as we sit and eat our roast beef together.

'Not really. Quite a few drunken guests falling over, and I've had the occasional person vomiting. Including a groom.'

'Alcohol or nerves?'

'Nerves. Well, I think it was nerves. None of that stuff ever makes it into the final film, obviously. I have had a bride and groom ask me to re-edit their video once, because in the background one of the bridesmaids can be seen in the distance snogging a married man. I didn't even notice it at the time, but they did, and wanted the evidence destroyed before it got out there.'

'Ha, and I take it you've never had to film any no-shows in the ceremony, or people objecting to the wedding?'

'Thankfully no, but there have been some moments when I've thought that a wedding was not going to go ahead. Grooms are always very conscious before the ceremony of how they are looking. They don't want to appear flustered or nervous to the guests, and they know that I've got a video camera pointed at them, so they try to put on a brave face. But they forget that they have a lapel microphone attached and that I can hear everything.'

'Oh no. What have you heard?'

'All sorts. I had one groom who started whispering to his best man that he didn't think he could go ahead with the wedding.'

'Why not?'

'I guess he got cold feet. This was at the front of the church, just a few minutes before the bride was due to arrive. The best man took the groom aside into the vestry and I heard the whole conversation with the groom saying he thought that maybe he shouldn't be getting married and the best man trying his hardest to persuade him.'

'What happened?'

'It was horrible. Eventually the groom agreed to go ahead with it. He came out and acted like nothing had happened. The bride arrived and everything continued as planned.'

'Did the groom ever realise that you had heard his conversation?'

'I don't know. When I went to take his microphone off him outside the church, there was a very brief look of panic in his eyes, but he was caught up in the occasion by that point. I've no idea if they are still together.'

'Those hidden microphones must be a nightmare. I bet loads of people forget.'

'They do. Especially after the speeches. I've heard all sorts of stuff. The worst was a bride who was giving a speech, so she had a microphone hidden in her dress. Then after they had done the toasts at the end of the speeches, the bride disappeared to the toilet. I think she must have had a dodgy stomach.'

'Oh shit, no!'

'Oh shit yes! That's something you don't want to hear.'

The roast beef is particularly tasty. We finish our plates and the caterer even brings us a bowl of sticky toffee pudding before the guests are served theirs. What a way to end my wedding photography career.

As with most other elements of the wedding, couples hugely overthink the catering. Yes, the meal is undoubtedly an important part of the day [*insert another joke about the colour scheme*], but it doesn't have to be fancy. As soon as the word 'wedding' is mentioned to a caterer, prices have a mysterious way of being gigantically inflated. Rachel and I wanted a simple pig roast at our wedding. We knew a local company that provided affordable pig roasts for events, but when we approached them for a quote and foolishly mentioned the 'W' word, and after all of the extras like plates, cutlery and a few salads were added on, the meal was suddenly fine-dining price.

So we ended up with a sit down meal provided by some very efficient, but slightly terrifying caterers – the same ones who objected to the receiving line at my friends' wedding. On the day before our wedding, the caterers got into a heated argument with the company providing our marquee because the caterers believed the quality of table they had been provided with in the kitchen marquee was sub-standard. Rather than asking if it was possible to get a different table, the caterer began shouting angrily at the marquee man, who was almost reduced to tears. He told me that in 25 years of doing marquees he had never been spoken to like that. It took a lot of persuading by my best men and me to keep him from going home and taking his marquee with him. I didn't dare mess with the caterers the day before our wedding. Despite their brashness, the food was fantastic and the service excellent.

But I have been to plenty of weddings where the food has been less glamorous and the service haphazard. And neither made the wedding any less enjoyable. A good friend of mine doesn't eat vegetables. He particularly hates anything green. For his wedding – a swanky black-tie event in a posh manor house – his mum and a few willing relatives cooked sausage, mashed potato and baked beans for 100 guests. It was one of the best wedding meals I've ever eaten.

Buffets can work out much cheaper as you are not paying for the same level of staffing. But bear in mind that it can be time-consuming for all your guests to queue up and fill their plates.

Served buffets – with a couple of joints of meat and a selection of salads – work very well as a compromise.

I have seen all sorts of other creative catering choices at weddings: pie and mash, fish and chips, pizza ovens, Caribbean barbeques, curries, afternoon tea. But there was one thing that tied together the different meal options at every single wedding I ever photographed. The guests were happy. I never once saw anybody complaining about their food. A free meal – whatever form it comes in – will always be appreciated. If you provided all your guests with a simple cheese sandwich, they would be happy. Apart from those damn vegans (joke!).

The best dessert I have ever seen was done in the form of a bake-off. The bride and groom had asked a group of their friends and family to bring a cake, if they wanted to. Some brought a simple sponge, some brought shop-bought offerings – including a very popular Colin the Caterpillar – and others went for a full-on showstopper challenge. The cakes were all laid out on a table, and the guests could fill their faces. There was more than enough for everyone, and it hadn't cost the bride and groom a penny. There is no reason this couldn't be done for the main course too, and your wedding breakfast could be one giant bring-your-own picnic.

FOURTEEN

I finish my dessert and then poke my head next door to see what stage of the meal they are all at. As the staff begin to clear away the plates and fill up the champagne flutes, I take my place at the back of the room for the speeches. The room is narrow enough for me to get great shots of all those speaking, without being in the way of any guests. Jayden has one video camera set up on a tripod at the edge of the room, and he is hand-holding another on his shoulder next to me.

For many – including me – the speeches are the highlight of a wedding. If you are one of the people tasked with doing a speech, it can be the worst part of the day and the cause of many months of anxiety.

If public speaking fills you with fear, you should know that you will never get an easier crowd than a wedding party. The audience are all on your side, they are friends and family of the bride and groom, they want to be entertained, they know you're scared, and they will laugh and smile to help you through it. And they will mostly all be drunk. In the world of public speaking, as daunting as it may seem, there honestly is no easier gig.

Traditionally, there are three speeches at a wedding: the father of the bride, the groom, and the best man. This tradition still largely stands, but there are often variations. Sometimes the father of the bride might not be at the wedding, sometimes the bride will have two dads, sometimes a mother or mother-in-law will want to speak, or the father of the groom, and sometimes the bride will do a speech too.

Jen and Matt have the three standard speeches planned, and Jen has said that depending on how she's feeling, she might say a few words at the end.

First up is Dave, the father of the bride. This is a speech I have not yet had to do, but as a father of two daughters, there is a good chance I will have to at some point in the future, so I will have to remember to practice what I preach.

If you are given this task, do say how proud of your daughter you are – even if you aren't. Tell her she looks beautiful on her wedding day – even if she doesn't. Say you are delighted that so-and-so is now officially a part of the family – even if he's a dick. And say how certain you are that they will be happy together for the rest of their lives – even if you secretly think you'll be making another father of the bride speech in a few years' time.

It's good to tell some funny stories about the bride growing up. You are allowed to take the mick out of her – she won't mind, or at least she shouldn't. Don't mention the amount of money you have had to fork out for this bloody wedding. Don't criticise the couple's ridiculously extravagant taste in venue/caterers/flowers. Don't get too drunk before your speech. This might be the only time in your life you get to publicly talk about your daughter. Don't fuck it up.

Don't get too sentimental about 'losing' your daughter. You are not losing her. She will still be your daughter. I have seen many fathers go on about this way too much and it comes across as possessive and slightly creepy. Instead of talking about losing your daughter, highlight the fact that you're gaining a son-in-law. It puts a much nicer spin on it. There's a commonly used line that works well – particularly if the groom is a tradesman – that goes something like… *'it doesn't feel like I am losing a daughter, it feels like I am gaining an electrician.'* This joke doesn't work so well if your new son-in-law is a Data Information Officer. Or a colorectal surgeon. Although, maybe that one does work. You could say he is a pain in the arse. *Ba dum tss!*

Showing a few photos of the bride as a child is effective. But don't use it as an excuse to reminisce about her entire life. I photographed one wedding where the father of the bride opened his speech with a picture of his daughter as a new-born baby. The crowd all made the correct *oohs* and *aahs*. He then talked the guests through those first few days, including way too much gory detail about the difficult birth. He showed another photo of the bride a few days old, loosely tied in to some other irrelevant story – possibly her first poo. Then another photo to show her moving on to solid foods, learning to crawl, learning to walk, her first holiday. I kept expecting there to be a miraculous time hop and his speech to rapidly catch up to present day. But he seemed to be recounting the bride's entire life… in real time. After the 65th slide I had lost the will to live. Many of the guests died during the time it took him to finish his speech, the bride and groom both aged significantly and there were several births.

In total, his speech, which was almost all a slideshow of photos of the bride growing up, lasted an hour and twenty minutes. Don't be that dad.

Jen's dad Dave gets the tone just right. He is funny, kind and sincere. It's the sort of speech I would love to be able to emulate one day. He seems like a different man to the dad who was hiding in the garage earlier this morning.

Next up is Matt. Despite his nerves at the pub earlier today, it's clear from the time I have spent with Matt that he will be absolutely fine.

The groom's speech is probably the easiest of the main speeches. Surrounded by all your friends and family, there is no expectation for you to be funny or entertaining. All you need to do is stand up and say a few thank yous and your captive audience will lap it up.

By all means make a few jokes. Following your speech, your best man will no doubt try his best to humiliate you, so why not strike a couple of early blows before he gets a chance. Unless the bride is also planning on saying a few words, it will be up to you to thank those people who were instrumental in either organising the wedding or in helping the two of you become a couple: parents, bridesmaids, best men, ushers, grandparents and perhaps even a toast to 'absent friends'. But whoever you thank, the most important person to mention in your speech is your new wife.

My best friend Damian – who claims his grandma invented banoffee pie – unfortunately missed this important memo during his speech at his wedding. Well, that's not strictly true. He knew he was supposed to talk about his wife. He even had a beautiful heartfelt tribute to her written down – he's a very caring and sensitive husband – but due to his nerves and being overwhelmed by the occasion, he forgot to read this part during his speech. He thanked his parents. He thanked his best men. He thanked the bridesmaids and the rest of the bridal party. He thanked the band, who hadn't even started performing. He thanked the caterers for cooking such an awesome beef wellington – it was particularly good and fully deserving of a mention. He thanked the florist – she wasn't even there. He thanked the photographer. He thanked the suit hire company. He even thanked the company that provided the portable toilets. But he didn't mention his wife.

We all sat there as he reeled off his long list of thank yous, building up to the big finish where he would start gushing about his beautiful wife Liz. Only he didn't. The speech ended, Liz put on a smile, as did the rest of the guests – some of whom hadn't noticed, but most had – and he sat down.

Ten years later and they are still happily married. It doesn't come up in conversation very often. Only like every time I see him. The fact that I am now putting it in print isn't going to help matters. I think Liz secretly likes it, though, as it is a trump card she can play at any time for the rest of her life.

'Remember that time when we got married and you didn't even mention me?'

As predicted, Matt nails his speech and hands over to James, his best man.

There is more expectation from guests for the best man's speech than any of the others. That's not to say it must be anything special. As I said before, you will never ever have an easier opportunity to make people laugh. You only need to watch a selection of best man speeches on YouTube to see that drunken wedding guests will laugh at absolutely anything.

People will expect you to ridicule the groom a little. But don't go overboard with this. You want to remain friends after the wedding. It's fine to tell a couple of funny stories, but if these stories do too much to lessen the character of the groom then you have taken it too far. I have photographed weddings where the best man has basically laid in to the groom for a full half an hour, exposing all sorts of inappropriate exploits with previous girlfriends and stories about the stag do that should have definitely stayed on the stag do. The groom did his best to laugh along but you could tell he was fuming inside, and there were some heated arguments between the groom and best man (and bride and groom) later that evening.

There is a bit of an art to giving a good best man speech. You must try and find that line between being funny and sincere but without crossing the mark and becoming a dick. If you are not a naturally funny person and uncomfortable going with a comedy speech, then a few genuine words about the bride and groom will be perfectly adequate.

What there is no excuse for is a best man's speech with absolutely no thought or effort put into it. I've seen best men stand up and say, 'yeah… err… thanks to Aaron for asking me to be his best man. Let's raise our glasses to the happy couple, yeah.' And then that's it. I've stood there, anticipating this to be part of an act and surely the best man would then launch into his proper speech, but then I have realised that was his speech. I've seen another speech where the best man has stood up and said, 'I haven't really got anything to say, except… Cheers!'

I have also been at weddings where the best man has categorically refused to say anything at all. Now, these weren't best men suffering from chronic anxiety and nerves about public speaking. They were simply men who couldn't give a damn about what an honour it was for them to be given the role of best man. It doesn't matter if you are funny or confident, all that matters is that you at least make a bit of effort. If you are a best man, given the task of making a speech at a wedding, you should consider it a real privilege. Out of all the men present at the wedding, you are the one considered by the bride and groom to be the 'best'. If you can't even muster a few words, what does that say about the rest of the men at the wedding?

There is nothing wrong with recycling some jokes you found on sample speeches on the internet. Jokes that get repeated from speech to speech are done so because they are genuinely funny, or at least corny enough to raise a smile. And not all of the guests will have heard them before. And those that have will still laugh. There is something nice about the familiarity and predictability of jokes in wedding speeches. There are certain jokes that I would hear at almost every wedding *(It's such an emotional day. Even the cake is in tiers.' 'I hope Steve and Caroline enjoy their honeymoon in North Wales. Well, I think it was North Wales. Steve said he was going to Bangor for a week.' 'This is not the first time today I've stood up from a warm seat with a piece of paper in my hand.)* Despite having heard these same lines repeated countless times, I still smiled at the thought of the best man googling *'best wedding speech in the world ever'*.

Don't make it a one-way street of jokes and abuse. Say something nice about the groom and say something equally nice about the bride. Make sure everyone knows you consider it an honour to be best man. If you don't put some effort in to show you are worthy, you won't be the groom's best man after the wedding.

James takes the microphone and begins.

'There comes a time in a person's life when you meet your one true love. That special someone who knows and understands you. A kindred spirit. Your soulmate...'

All eyes turn to Jen and Matt, who gaze lovingly at each other. Matt takes Jen's hand and gives it a squeeze.

James continues... 'That moment came for Matt, 17 years ago... when he met me.'

The crowd – led by Jen and Matt – all erupt into laughter, and James continues his high standard of speech right the way through to the end.

The hug that Jen and Matt give James afterwards shows what a brilliant job he has done.

When I first started out in wedding photography, the bride's speech was a rarity. By the time I hung up my photography bag for good, it was much more commonplace. I really liked it when the bride did a speech. Occasionally, the bride would have prepared a full speech, but more often than not, she would take the microphone and say a few impromptu words, mostly thanking everyone for coming and sharing the day with them.

I have seen brides who appear to be the most timid and reserved people I've ever seen, suddenly come to life during the wedding breakfast when they realise they are surrounded by all their friends and family, they've had a couple of glasses of champagne, and I've thought that they might never let go of the microphone.

Jen takes the microphone to briefly reiterate Matt's thank yous to everyone for coming and for making their day so special. It's clear that Jen and Matt's wedding day has exceeded all their expectations. I squash the camera closer to my face to hide the fact my eyes are welling up.

The wedding speeches usually come at the end of the meal. It gives the guests something to look forward to, and it provides a nice bit of entertainment before the often-prolonged gap until the evening reception.

There are some disadvantages, though. It makes the meal less enjoyable for all those who will be speaking. They will be unable to relax properly until after their speech and will often sit and pick at their food throughout, feeling too queasy to fully indulge. They might also try to calm their nerves with alcohol, and after an extended two-hour meal, during which little food is consumed, they might be completely wasted by the time it comes around to their speech. I saw one best man who was politely told to sit down mid-speech because he was slurring his words so much that he was completely incoherent.

Many couples now break with tradition and have the speeches first. This allows those that are speaking to get the stressful bit out of the way and then they can relax for the rest of the day. The disadvantage is that there is then nothing for the guests to look forward to at the end of the meal, and no entertaining interlude before the evening reception.

Here's what I suggest. Split the speeches. This is what Rachel and I did at our wedding and it worked a treat. Rachel's dad and I did our speeches before the meal, allowing us to enjoy our food without the worry of our impending speech. My best men were forced to wait until the end of the meal to do theirs. It was a little unfair on them, but I sold it to them that the guests would be a lot more inebriated by the end of the meal and would laugh more at their jokes.

Whatever you decide, make sure you tell your caterers. If you launch into impromptu speeches at the start of the meal when they had been expecting them at the end, you will have cold food which will most likely have been spat in.

At the end of Jen's speech, she raises another toast, this time to everyone. Everyone stands and clinks their glasses together. I had always believed this tradition of clinking glasses was based on a symbol of acknowledging that you trusted the person had not poisoned your drink. Rather than swapping glasses to make sure, you simply touch glasses to demonstrate your trust. I like this theory and the fact that the tradition continues today as though poisoning is still rife at modern social gatherings.

There is, however, little evidence to back this theory up. It is considered more likely that the practice of clinking glasses originates from the time when groups of people shared the same vessel for drinking. As societies developed and became more prosperous, they were able to acquire their own cups. Having previously drunk together, they would then clink vessels together as a symbol that they were still united. Let's stick with the poison story, though. It's much better.

The reason it is called a toast is a little more interesting. For hundreds of years, when wine was not of the same quality it is today, pieces of spiced, toasted bread were placed in glasses of wine, partly to absorb some of the acidity of the cheap wine, and partly to impart some of the spices from the bread to improve the flavour. Surely this is another neglected wedding tradition that needs to make a comeback?

'So will you please be upstanding, sprinkle some spicy croutons into your wine, and raise a toast to the bride and groom.'

The person in charge of this process was known as the Master of the Toast, and so became what we know today as the Toastmaster.

I worked with many wedding toastmasters over the years, and I never met a single one that was actually useful. Wedding toastmasters, in their ridiculous red coats, white gloves, and their smug medal around their neck awarded to them for completing their 'training' – whatever that entails – are almost always men, approaching or past retirement age. They mean well, and their intentions are good, but they are bloody useless. They just get in the way and cause far more bother than good. Most wedding venues have their own wedding coordinator, or there will be someone that can liaise with the bridal party to tell them when it's time to sit down to eat. Having a toastmaster just adds an unnecessary additional cog to an already functioning machine. Everything slows down when a toastmaster is involved. Far from making things more efficient, a toastmaster complicates the fuck out of everything.

Imagine the scene. The caterers are ready for people to come and sit down to eat, they pass the message on to one of the ushers, who happens to have a particularly loud voice. The usher is just about to stand on a chair and shout '*grub's up, everyone. Please go and take your seats.'* But then one of the quieter and meeker ushers taps him on the shoulder and reminds him that Stan, the toastmaster, has to call people through to the wedding breakfast. In fact, that is Stan's only job.

But where the hell is Stan? Stan has gone AWOL. After a quick hunt around the venue, Stan is located in the carpark having an argument on the phone with his ex-wife. He's told his moment has arrived.

'Ok,' says Stan. 'I'll be right with you.'

Five minutes later, Stan emerges and then remembers he has forgotten his bugle.

'You don't need a bugle, Stan,' says the usher. 'I can just shout for you to get people's attention if you like.'

'No,' says Stan, 'I need my bugle. It's part of my schtick. I'll be right back.'

Stan waddles off to his car and returns five minutes later with his completely pointless bugle.

He then asks one of the ushers to go and get him a glass of water to lubricate his throat, while he makes strange coughing noises in the meantime, which are either part of his vocal warm up routine or symptoms of a chronic lung condition.

The water finally arrives, and Stan starts gargling – a tune I recognise but can't quite place – before standing on his chair and blowing his bugle for a full breath. Aunt Joan spills her drink in shock, Grandad Arnold nearly has a heart attack, one of the bride's young nieces starts crying. But Stan has certainly got the guests' attention. Rather than just telling the assembled crowd to go through and take their seats, Stan unrolls an elegant and completely unnecessary scroll and launches into an elaborate and over-the-top speech, talking aimlessly about love and marriage, food and celebration ('A *bit like your book, George,'* I hear you say. Pipe down!). By the time the guests have made their way through to their seats, 20 minutes have passed since the usher was about to shout, '*grub's up*' and the end result would have been exactly the same, only without the now irate caterers cursing the toastmaster for making the food go cold.

One of the job requirements of being a toastmaster is that you must love the sound of your own voice. In fact, I think that is the only requirement. So, toastmasters milk this at every opportunity they get. And they like to use this position of authority to control the wedding and complicate an otherwise uncomplicated situation. Fortunately, toastmasters are a dying breed. Thank fuck for that.

FIFTEEN

I feel a little emotional. The speeches often have this effect on me but nothing like today. You learn a lot about the bride and groom during wedding speeches and I'm often surprised by what I hear. I photographed one groom who was a quiet, reserved accountant. During the best man speech, I learned that the groom had recently swam the English Channel (an achievement accomplished by fewer people than have climbed Mount Everest). Out of all the guests at the wedding, the groom was possibly the person I least expected to have swum the English Channel.

I learned about a bride who was fluent in seven languages. I learned about a groom who had recently gone into remission after several years battling cancer. I learned about a bride whose wedding fell in the middle of a course of chemotherapy. I learned about a bride and groom who were getting married one week before their final exams at medical school – they met during fresher's week and were about to graduate together as doctors.

I will no doubt see many more wedding speeches in my life, but I will miss this unique opportunity to learn more about two people I feel like I know, but actually don't know at all.

And I've genuinely liked every one of my wedding couples. Preparing to get married can certainly bring out the worst in people, but by the end of the wedding day it usually brings out the best. I had plenty of brides and grooms that were slightly difficult and high-maintenance during the build up to the wedding, but even the most challenging of brides managed to win me over in the end.

Louise was like no other bride I ever photographed. From my first conversation with her I was terrified. She was a corporate lawyer and lived and worked in New York with her fiancé Ian. She was getting married in Northampton but was doing all the organising from the other side of the Atlantic via phone and email. We had several phone conversations and sent emails back and forth while she was deciding on her photographer, and the more I spoke to her, the more I hoped she would decide not to book me. She viewed her wedding as another corporate deal, and every interaction was ruthless and business-like. She eventually agreed to hire me – much to my disappointment – and I sent her the contract to sign. I didn't hear back from her for a few months and then she contacted me to tell me her budget wasn't as big as they had originally thought, and could I reduce my rates. I knew the package I offered was one of the most competitive around so politely said no. She signed the contract.

She would send me random emails asking for me to recommend videographers, or wedding singers. I always replied straightaway (I was too scared not to) with a list of people for her to get in touch with. Each time, she would then contact me again a few days later, slightly angrily asking why I had not responded. I would forward my original reply to her showing that I had replied, and she would say something like, '*oh, totally snowed here.*'

She used to call our landline in the middle of the night, and when I answered the phone sounding surprised and perhaps a little irritated, she would just say, '*Oh, I keep forgetting about the time difference.*'

We eventually met face to face a few months before the wedding when they were back in the country. She was every bit as scary as I feared. Her fiancé, Ian, was nice enough but he had absolutely no interest in sorting out the details of the day and was happy for Louise to take the lead. If he had been interested, there would have been no chance Louise would have allowed him a say anyway.

'Now listen here, George. I've got something really important to say,' she said.

'Ok.'

'I only want you to photograph me from my left side.'

'Ok… really?'

'Yes. Just the left side.'

'Right….'

'No, I said left!'

'But you will look fantastic.'

'You're not listening. I don't want you to photograph the right side of my face. It doesn't photograph well. Trust me.'

'Ok…'

'And I don't like my arms. So please try and avoid having them in photographs. I know that they will be visible in some of them, but please don't take many pictures of me with my arms showing.'

'Got it. Anything else?'

'It would be great if we could have our photos converted to sepia. I really like sepia. And you know those photos that are black and white but with a bit of colour in them?'

'Colour drop?'

'Yeah, colour drop. I LOVE colour drop. If you could do some colour drop photos that would be fab.'

'Well… I…'

'And the venue doesn't usually open the bridal suite until 10 a.m. but I've managed to persuade them to open it at 7.30 a.m. especially for me, so I would like you to be there before I arrive. I'll probably be arriving in my PJ bottoms so don't get any photos of those.'

'But…'

'Just the top half of me. I'll probably be wearing a jumper.'

'Is it ok to photograph your arms when you're wearing a jumper?'

'I suppose so. Not too many photos, though. But it would be good for you to get some photos of me arriving to see the smile on my face when I see the venue.'

'The smile on your face just from the left side?'

I was worried I had overstepped the mark, but she responded with, 'Very good, you're paying attention. Just the left side.'

I knew the venue staff well and it turned out Louise was using a florist and makeup artist I had worked with many times. For the months leading up to the wedding, we all compared notes on the random demands Louise had given us – from the particular shade of pink roses in the bouquet, to the exact length of the stems on the floral arrangements on the tables, to how the makeup had to be applied with a specific piece of music playing in the background, and the eyeshadow had to be applied differently on the right side of her face to the left. Not that it mattered because I wouldn't be photographing that side anyway. We were all half dreading Louise's wedding, but also slightly excited about what was going to happen.

The day itself got off to a particularly bad start. I was at the venue nice and early as requested. Louise arrived looking even more focused and intense than I was expecting. And by focused and intense, I mean terrifying and psychotic. She wore a pair of sunglasses that were so big they covered most of her face – the good and the bad side. The rest of her face was taken up by a massive scowl. I let her get set up in the bridal suite and then walked in as she was barking orders at the makeup artist, who was very calmly trying to reassure Louise that it was definitely the same foundation brush she had used in the makeup trial. The florist cowered in the corner with Louise's bouquet, nervous about whether it would meet her impossibly high standards.

'George, I don't think this is going to work out,' said Louise, after I had taken my first picture.

'What do you mean?' I said.

'I can't do this right now.'

'Sorry, can't do what?'

'Deal with this makeup crisis and have my photo taken.'

'Ok, that's fine. I'll go and get some photos around the venue. Shall I come back in about 15 minutes?'

'No. To be honest, I don't really want you to shoot me now.'

'I wish someone would shoot me now,' I muttered.

'What was that?'

'Er… nothing. Are you sure? You look great already. I'm only photographing your left side.'

'Yes. I'll give you a shout in a couple of hours when I'm ready.'

'Ok, if you're sure.'

'I'm sure.'

The makeup artist and florist exchanged glances with me as I left the room. They both had the expression of, '*Help!* P*lease don't leave us here alone in the lion's den,*' and I had the look of, '*sorry, ladies, it's every man for himself. I'm going to get the hell out of here before I get mauled to death.*'

So, I went and got a coffee and read the paper for a couple of hours. It was one of the nicest morning's work I had ever had.

The moment Louise was in her dress she was like a totally different person. This was the moment she had been preparing for. Up until this point, there were always jobs she could be doing, things she should be checking, demands she could be making. All the stresses and anxieties of her big day that had manifested into this hideous bridezilla character, melted away

184

once she transitioned from a wedding planner to a bride. Now was her time to enjoy the day.

She was absolutely delightful for the rest of the wedding. My day was admittedly a little challenging, trying to only photograph her on the left side and tightly cropping all the photos so her arms weren't visible, but it made the experience all the more memorable.

I usually received payment for my wedding photography four weeks before the wedding, but due to some mix-up with an international bank transfer, Louise didn't pay me before the wedding. I had been too scared of her to protest. After the wedding, I had nothing to fear, so I held off sending her the photos until she paid me in full – which she eventually did two months later. I never did the sepia or the colour drop.

SIXTEEN

Rachel and I had three children together during my time as a wedding photographer, and there was a fair amount of worry about one of them being born on the day I was working. I made the decision not to tell any of my wedding couples – either at the pre-wedding meeting, or on their wedding day – that my wife was heavily pregnant and due to go into labour at any moment. I didn't think it would do much to aid their pre-wedding anxiety levels. Instead, I kept a list of phone numbers for about a dozen other wedding photographers in my camera bag, and if anything happened on the day, I planned to start phoning around frantically trying to get someone to cover for me.

Layla, our first child, was born on a Wednesday in June. I had a couple of weddings that month, but fortunately she avoided them. What I hadn't taken into consideration was the scattering of other photography jobs I had been booked for. Layla was born at 9 a.m. at home. We had a lovely, if not surreal first day, trying to get our heads around the idea we were now responsible for this brand-new life. It was late afternoon when I suddenly remembered I was supposed to be photographing the official opening of a housing development on the other side of Northampton. With no time to find a replacement, and with Rachel and my new daughter Layla both fast asleep, I drove across town, took some photos of people toasting champagne glasses and cutting a ribbon – all the while in a complete daze – and returned home before they had even woken up.

Leo, our second child, was due in December, and I only had a couple of bookings that month too. He arrived on a Thursday and the bride and groom at the wedding I photographed two days later knew nothing of the fact I hadn't slept in 72 hours and was far from fully functioning.

Our youngest daughter Kitty was more problematic. She was due in August. An August in which I had nine weddings booked. My busiest month ever. I was so paranoid about Kitty's birth that I contacted several other wedding photographers during the weeks before to let them know the situation and make a note of the dates of their availability. I obviously couldn't expect these photographers to remain on standby without compensation, so did not view my backup list as a failsafe solution, but it was at least a step towards having a contingency plan.

Kitty was born on a Saturday. A Saturday in August.

Someone was smiling down on me that day (presumably not God, unless he had forgiven me for missing all the reading of the banns at our wedding. Or maybe he's a big football fan and understood that my team needed me?). Kitty was born on the only Saturday in that August that I didn't have a wedding. I had wedding bookings on the Friday and the Sunday – both of which I photographed – but she arrived slap bang in the middle of the two.

You can't phone in sick as a wedding photographer. There were several weddings that if I had been working another job, I would have taken the day off without a second thought. On one occasion, I felt so bad that I genuinely didn't think I was going to make it through the wedding. I felt nauseous all day, my legs had turned to jelly, and I found it a real struggle just to stand up. I couldn't eat a mouthful of the delicious-looking food the caterers brought me. During the speeches, in the warm and crowded wedding breakfast room, I started sweating profusely. I found an empty seat and sat down, keeping my camera raised to my eye, to help shield my clammy face.

As the guests clapped the end of the groom's speech, I made a quick dash for the door and the cool of the open air. But my stomach still wasn't happy. I ran the length of the courtyard and into the carpark where I vomited violently into a bush. I drank some water, rinsed my mouth out, gathered my composure and went back into the room to photograph the best man's speech.

I took fewer than half the number of photos I usually take at a wedding. But the couple were very happy with their photos and didn't notice anything was wrong. I usually give the bride and groom a hug each at the end of the night, but on this occasion, I kept my distance, so they didn't spend their honeymoon spewing into a hedge.

Jen and Matt's guests are politely asked to vacate the room so that the staff can start preparing for the evening reception. The band have arrived and have all their gear stacked up outside and ready to bring in as soon as the room is clear.

'Those were really great speeches, both of you. Well done,' I say to Jen and Matt.

'Thanks,' says Matt. 'I'm glad it's over.'

'I bet. Brilliant speech, James,' I say to the best man as he walks past. 'I thought you did a cracking job. It was one of the best I've heard.'

'Thanks. I bet you say that to everyone.'

'I honestly don't. If it's bad – and I've seen some truly terrible speeches – I don't say anything at all. You were all brilliant.'

'Thanks. I appreciate that,' says James. 'I'm off to the bar. Can I get you a drink?'

'Not for me thanks. I've got a long drive home.'

'Where have you got to drive to?'

'Devon,' I say.

'Devon? Are you serious? You've got to drive to bloody Devon tonight?'

'He moved there just after we booked him,' says Jen. 'To tell you the truth, Matt and I were a bit worried you wouldn't turn up.'

'Of course I was going to turn up,' I say.

'We are relieved you did. Thanks for doing such a great job today,' says Jen. 'You've been brilliant.'

'You haven't seen the photos yet!'

'I'm sure they will be fantastic. When will we get to see them?'

'They will be waiting for you when you get back from your honeymoon.' I want to tell them this is my last wedding, but it doesn't feel right. 'Where did you say you were going for your honeymoon? The Maldives?'

'Yeah,' says Matt. 'Kindly paid for by our wedding guests. We're flying tomorrow evening. Can't wait.'

'You lucky bastards,' says James. 'I've got to go back to work on Monday.'

I believe that the honeymoon is one of the most important parts of a wedding. And yes, I do see it as part of a wedding. A honeymoon doesn't need to be an exotic, luxurious trip to some far-flung paradise island, though. It just needs to be a chance for the newly wedded couple to enjoy some quality time together at the start of their married life. And no, I am not putting quotation marks around the phrase quality time. I mean it purely in a non-sexual way. Well, mostly.

As previously mentioned, instead of presents, Rachel and I gave friends and family the option of contributing to our honeymoon fund. The following year, we spent six incredible weeks in South America, wading through swamps searching for

189

anacondas, piranha fishing in the Bolivian jungle and trying to get to Machu Picchu (read all about it in my book, *Travels with Rachel: In Search of South America*). But we also understood the importance and need for a break immediately after our wedding, so we booked a last-minute package holiday to Corfu. Rachel still thinks we went to Crete for our honeymoon. It was definitely Corfu. We have never been to Crete. We did very little during the week, and rarely ventured beyond the hotel, but it was important for us to spend that quality time (again, no quotation marks) together to remind us why we got married.

During our honeymoon, I thought it would be a romantic gesture to draw a big love heart in sun cream on my stomach. Rachel didn't seem particularly enamoured by my efforts, but I left it there in the hope it would win her affection. After an hour lying in the sun, I was left with a big white heart shape when the rest of my body had turned pink. It attracted sniggers from all those I walked past. The following day, I tried to correct it by applying sun cream everywhere except the heart, but this resulted in severe heart-shaped sunburn instead.

A surprising number of couples I photographed either didn't go on honeymoon or planned to maybe have a honeymoon later in the year or the following year. Sometimes there were genuine reasons, like the couple were doctors or teachers and couldn't arrange time off work – even then I did wonder if they couldn't have scheduled the wedding for a time when they could have followed it with a short break.

'*I couldn't get any more time off work,*' said another bride, after she had just got back from two weeks in Malaga on an extended hen do.

But money was always the main factor.

'*We spent so much on the wedding we just can't afford to go away this year,*' they would say, taking a sip of the Moët & Chandon champagne they had insisted on serving to their guests, because '*prosecco just simply doesn't cut it.*'

I would look around at the extravagant floral arrangements, or the unnecessary table decorations they had bought for the wedding and wonder if that was all really more important than some time away together after the wedding.

Book a honeymoon. Even if it's just a couple of nights in a Travelodge on the M25, you need to get away for a few days. Organising a wedding is a big undertaking and if you crash straight back down into real life without any relaxing transition period, you are destined for trouble. A 2014 academic study by Andrew Francis-Tan and Hugo M. Mialon – called, topically, *A Diamond Is Forever* – concluded that there was a lower risk of divorce for couples who opt to go on honeymoon.

As you will have come to expect during this book, not all wedding traditions have romantic origins. The honeymoon is no exception. Some historians believe the honeymoon came about as a way for the groom to take his bride into hiding after a kidnapped wedding. During this time, the bride's family would eventually give up looking for her, and after this time away, the bride would likely fall pregnant making it far harder for the wedding to be annulled.

Another theory, which sounds a bit more fun, is that the honeymoon originated from the 5th century custom of the guests giving mead – the alcoholic drink made from honey – as an offering to the newly-married couple. The mead was supposed to increase fertility, so the bride and groom would then spend a moon cycle – so almost an entire month – getting drunk and enjoying some 'quality time' together.

'I'm very jealous too,' I say. 'I'm sure you'll have an amazing time in The Maldives.'

'Are you sure I can't get you a drink from the bar? Soft drink? Coffee?' says James.

'No, I'm honestly fine. Thanks very much.'

I was offered countless drinks at every wedding I ever photographed. Being surrounded all day by people drinking alcohol from the moment I arrived in the morning, to the moment I left at night, it was always tempting to have a beer or a glass of wine and join in the celebrations – many other wedding suppliers I worked with happily accepted – but I chose not to. I knew I wouldn't be able to fully relax until I was back home, and the photos were all backed up on my computer. I would then sit down for a beer and my shish kebab and chips bought from Embers Grill takeaway at the end of our road. If everything had gone to plan, and I had left the wedding on time, this would be in time for *Match of the Day* at 10.30 p.m. That was when I was living in Northampton. Now that we lived in Devon, it was usually gone 3 a.m. by the time I climbed into bed. I always drove back to Devon straight after my Northampton weddings – unless I had another one that weekend – as I didn't want to spend too much time away from my family, and the roads were nice and quiet in the middle of the night. It was purely coincidental that my weekly game of Dads' football took place early on a Sunday morning.

Once my photos were safely backed up, I was able to relax. But until that moment, I was constantly paranoid of a technical problem during the wedding. I was confident in my own ability to get the photos I needed, but I didn't have the same confidence in my equipment. Technology failure – a faulty camera or corrupted memory card – was always a fear as it was something out of my control. All I could do was to try to minimise these risks and have a contingency plan in place should anything happen. I always carried two cameras. One on each shoulder. I had a camera bag of lenses that I would leave stashed behind a curtain or under a table during the wedding reception, but the cameras would never leave my person. This way, even if my camera bag was stolen, I would still have the equipment I needed to photograph the wedding. Both cameras had different lenses – one wide and one telephoto – and I would alternate them regularly, partly to get a good variety of shots, but also to ensure that if one memory card were to fail, I had adequate pictures on the other.

When I first started out, I used a stack of lower capacity memory cards. I would fill up one, and then switch to the next. My philosophy was that if one memory card became corrupted then it would only be a small portion of the day. I then learned that the most common time that a memory card becomes damaged is when it is being transferred in and out of a camera. Also, having multiple memory cards increased the likelihood of one or more of them being lost, stolen or damaged. From then on, I kept one large capacity memory card in each camera and didn't remove them until after the wedding.

I didn't have backups of all camera lenses, as some photographers recommend, but I had enough different lenses so that if one failed, I had adequate replacements that could get me through the rest of the day.

This is all probably boring as hell to anyone not interested in the technicalities of wedding photography – it's possibly boring as hell to those that are, too – but I feel like I'm releasing some of this pent-up anxiety by getting my worries out of my mind and onto the page.

During Jen and Matt's wedding – my final paid job as a photographer – these worries were heightened as though I had been riding my luck my whole career. But it was reassuring to know I would soon never again have to fret about a camera's shutter seizing, a lens breaking, or a memory card failing. All I had to do was get through these next few hours without a technical hitch and it would all be ok.

My nervousness and anxiety around equipment failure stems back from the hours I spent in the university darkroom developing my own photos, and the countless failures and mishaps along the way.

I am 'only' 39, but it's scary to think that many of you reading this book will not have any experience of using a film camera. You young photographers nowadays with your swanky digital cameras and your snazzy smartphones, you've got it so easy. You don't know how lucky you are.

For all you young'uns out there who don't know what a film camera is, allow me to enlighten you. Film cameras don't have a screen on the back for you to preview your photo. You don't know quite how shit your photos will look until the film has been developed. Most camera films comprised of 24 or 36 exposures and once these were all taken, the film was usually sent to a photo lab, where an automated process took care of the developing and turned your roll of film into physical prints. If you wanted the freedom to manipulate the photos in any way, then you had to develop them yourself. It wasn't a case of clicking a different filter or playing around with the levels in Photoshop, the process was a little more complicated than that.

I was given a very brief tutorial of the film developing process in the darkroom from a post-grad student at university, and then learned by trial and error. Mostly error.

The first stage of the process is by far the most difficult. Inside the plastic film cannister is a long roll of film containing your photos. Before you even begin to make prints, this has to be extracted from the small canister and wound carefully onto a reel before the chemical process begins. It's an extremely fiddly job, and to make things a little bit more challenging, you must do it in the dark. I'm not just talking about closing the curtains, I'm talking total fucking blackness. They don't call them dark rooms for nothing. If even a sliver of lights gets into the room, you're done for.

You get all your equipment lined up in advance, take a deep breath, and then flick the light switch. The top of the film cannister gets prised off with a can opener, often with the tool being dropped on the floor followed by a frantic search on your hands and knees to try and retrieve it. Then the film is carefully removed from the cannister, being mindful not to actually touch the surfaces because this too will ruin it. The film is cut free with a pair of scissors (which you probably drop multiple times too) and then the film will try and wrap itself around your arm like a mutant slinky. Staying calm and untangling the bloody thing from your arm, without actually touching it, and making sure it doesn't make contact with the floor or the work surfaces, you thread the end of it into a small plastic spool. This was the part I found most challenging. Still in complete darkness, the winding mechanism of the spool would often not work, I would start to get angry and frustrated and the two parts of the device would come apart or get stuck and not wind the film on.

After about half an hour of sweating and swearing, with the film successfully wound onto the spool, it is placed in a plastic container with a lid screwed tightly on. A series of chemicals are then added to this container, for a very specific amount of time, and the container gets lightly turned (or 'agitated' as they say in the trade), like you are a lazy cocktail bartender. The negatives are then washed and hung up to dry on a line for several hours. After this stage, your negatives are ready to make prints from.

The light can be switched on and you can breathe a sigh of relief. You still don't have any actual photos to show for your hard work, but you have the negatives from which the photos are made.

But it didn't always work out that way. More often than not, I would have some sort of problem during this crucial first stage. There were so many things that could and did go wrong. Sometimes the roll of film would spring from the canister like a possessed jack in the box onto the floor, or into a tray of chemicals. Sometimes the reel mechanism would fail completely, and the film would not be wound onto the spool correctly. There was no lock on the door to the dark room and although there was a light outside that signified the room was in use, people didn't always notice and would occasionally burst aimlessly into the room, spilling light onto the film and ruining the entire process.

Often, this would be a roll of film that I would have taken weeks to finish. Perhaps getting up before sunrise and walking or taking the bus to some nearby building or ruin to photograph it at first light. Sometimes I would have stayed up late, practising long exposures of the night sky. Or the film would contain portraits of friends and family, as I tried to hone my photography skills. With only 24 or 36 images to each film, every photo was precious and I carefully considered long and hard before clicking the shutter. Imagine after all this work and effort, that the film becomes ruined before even seeing a single photo.

It seems crazy to think that we put ourselves through that stress (and some film aficionados still do today) when we could have taken the film to a store to be processed. But the stress was part of the fun. It was about creating something. And the long, slow, arduous process of turning a film into prints was what gave me the photography bug. Snapping the photos was the easy part. By learning my trade with a film camera and in the darkroom, I gained a better understanding of photography, and a greater appreciation for every click of the shutter.

The first wedding I photographed was a favour for a friend. Digital SLRs didn't exist so I was using two film cameras – in one I was shooting black and white, in the other I was using colour. Colour and black and white films have very different developing processes. One of the black and white films I was using was a different brand, and confusingly had to be developed like a colour film, as it was basically a colour film, only without the colour. I wasn't brave enough to process and develop the wedding photos myself, so took my batch of films to a popular high-street photo lab. I made a point of specifically highlighting that this particular black and white film needed to be processed in a colour machine. The young lab assistant nodded at me, like I was patronising him, but I reiterated my point to make sure he knew. He rolled his eyes at me.

When I picked up the photos a week later, one of the set of negatives was completely blank and it was apparent that this film had been processed as a black and white film and totally ruined in the process. Thankfully, the other five or six films were processed correctly, and my friends would not have known about the missing photos had I not told them. The popular high-street photo lab (I don't want to name and shame them – ok, I do, it was Boots. Bloody Boots) tried to deny it was their fault, but eventually admitted responsibility and gave me a measly £2 gift voucher as compensation.

Digital photography carries far fewer risks than film, as damaged film stock or a faulty camera would often not be picked up until after a film was developed, and by that point it was obviously too late to rectify. With digital cameras, at least the photographer can check the photos on the camera's screen during the day to make sure there are no problems. But memory cards can get corrupted, and laptops can malfunction, which is why I always made backups as soon as I got home after the wedding.

Perhaps overly cautious, I would then hide my laptop away somewhere safe in the house and keep my memory cards with me in the bedroom, before making a second backup the following day. My extreme paranoia was brought about from a photographer friend of mine recounting a horror story of his own experience. He returned from a full day's wedding shoot and backed up the photos onto his laptop before going to bed that night. While he slept, his house was broken into, and both his laptop and his camera bag – containing all the memory cards – were stolen. The bride and groom were left without any photos of their wedding. To offer some compensation, my photographer friend ended up paying for suit hire, hair and makeup for the bridal party, and many of the group photos were recreated at a later date.

In over 250 weddings, I did have a couple of occasions with corrupted memory cards, but in each instance, I was able to salvage most of the lost photos using recovery software. Even without any technical problems, and a supposedly competent camera operator, it is still possible for human error to play a factor. On one occasion, I managed to mess up spectacularly because of my own stupidity.

Taking a photograph without a memory card inserted into the camera is possibly the most stupid mistake a photographer can make. It shouldn't even be possible, and on most cameras, there is a setting to ensure it can't happen. I had disabled this setting in my camera the previous day when I was checking one of my lenses and didn't have a card handy. I then forgot to re-enable it.

The following day, I was photographing a wedding. I had taken lots of photos throughout the ceremony and was approaching the maximum capacity for the memory card I was using so removed it. Immediately after the ceremony, the entire wedding party of about 80 guests was assembling at the bottom of some steps for a big group photo. It was at this stage I was supposed to put the new card in, but Uncle Melvin had started talking to me about camera lenses and wondering what advantages I thought the 24-105mm had over the 28-80mm, as though I gave a shit. I gathered everyone together, got them to look up at me with big expectant smiles, as I fired off a few photos. I told them all to wave a hand in the air and I said my '*if you're holding a drink, not that hand*', line. Then I glanced at the camera and the screen briefly displayed a lovely photo of all the wedding guests. I was confident I had the photos I needed, so, not wanting to hold up the celebrations any longer, I thanked the guests and they all began to disperse.

It was at this point I clicked on the *playback* button to have a more thorough look at the photos. To my horror, the screen displayed the words '*NO CARD INSERTED.*' I felt an instant surge of panic. Even without a memory card, I knew my camera still showed a quick preview of the photo on the screen for a couple of seconds, but *surely that wasn't what I had seen?*

'*I've never taken photos without a memory card,*' I thought to myself. '*No professional photographer would do something as stupid as that.*'

I pulled open the compartment door on the camera and my heart sank as I noticed there was no card inserted in the slot. *Oh fuckity fuckity fuck fuck!* I wanted to throw up. My heart raced. *What should I do? Call everyone back and tell them there has been a problem and I need to retake the photo?* Yes, this is what I probably should have done, but I looked around and many of the guests had already moved inside to visit the bathroom or bar, and others had congregated for a cigarette at the far end of the courtyard. One elderly gentleman who had been helped down the ramp into the courtyard, was now back up at the higher level and I couldn't possibly ask him to come back down again. So, I decided to ignore it. The big group shot was one of the most important photos of the day, but it was one I had offered to do and not something the bride and groom had specifically requested. I knew my photos from the rest of the day were very good, and we still had the group photos and couple photos to come. I would make sure I put a memory card in the camera for those.

I didn't say anything to the bride and groom until after their honeymoon and blamed it on a corrupted memory card, rather than an incompetent photographer. Fortunately, they were delighted with the rest of their photos and were happy to live without the big group shot. It's a mistake that you only ever make once.

SEVENTEEN

Jen and Matt have invited an additional 40 guests to the evening reception. They are mostly work friends and members of Jen's hockey team and Matt's 5-aside football team. Having photographed the same group of people all day, it's nice to see some fresh faces. It has been dark outside for a few hours, but there are candles, gas heaters, fairy lights in the trees, and spotlights illuminating the outside of the barns, making the venue look almost prettier at night than it did during the day.

The band are still setting up in the main barn. The temperature has dropped considerably since the sun set and almost everyone – apart from a few hardcore smokers – are chatting and drinking inside the other barn.

This lull in proceedings is the part of a wedding that tends to drag a bit, and couples often think of novel ways to amuse their guests. Photo-booths are popular, as are caricaturists, fancy dress boxes, pick-n-mix stands, chocolate fountains, casinos, magicians and musicians. All of these are fun and can add a bit of entertainment and originality to your wedding. But don't feel like people have to be stimulated for the duration of your wedding. The vast majority of your guests will be very happy to have a break and let the huge meal they've just eaten settle down before they start shaking their thang on the dancefloor. Those that are restless and unable to stay still will find ways to amuse themselves. During the wedding reception of one female civil partnership I photographed, an impromptu rugby match began between the two women's rugby teams that one of the couple played for. It was quite a spectacle. Another wedding I photographed turned into a giant cricket match involving most of the guests. The bride even took a turn at batting. During my own wedding, we played football on the grass outside the marquee for almost an hour after the meal. My best man twisted his ankle so badly that he had to do one-legged dancing for the rest of the night.

Once your band or DJ begin their set, you will want as many people as possible to be on that dancefloor. If the added entertainment you provide is too good and too distracting, all you will be doing is luring people away.

Fireworks are bizarrely popular at weddings. I've never understood it, to be honest. As if weddings aren't expensive enough, why not spend even more of your money and literally watch it burn in front of your eyes? Here's a moneysaving tip for you: don't waste money on fireworks at your wedding. Spend it on sugared almonds instead.

I photographed a wedding on November 5th and the bride and groom wanted to have a small firework display to acknowledge that their wedding was on Bonfire Night. The venue they had chosen would not allow fireworks due to some small print in their insurance, but, undeterred, the bride and groom made other plans. At about 7 p.m., during the lull in proceedings between the end of the wedding breakfast and the start of the evening do, two big buses turned up at the wedding venue. All the guests and I boarded the buses and we drove 15 minutes up the road to the village where the bride and groom lived. Everyone disembarked – the bride wearing wellies with her dress – and we watched the village's firework display for 20 minutes and then got the bus back to the venue.

When the bride and groom had told me this was going to be happening, I was a little cynical and thought that it seemed like an awful lot of effort for the sake of some fireworks, but it proved to be an extremely fun and welcome interlude to the day.

Sparklers are another popular wedding accessory during winter weddings. They can brighten up dark evenings and provide brief amusement during the proceedings. However, it's also worth noting that fire and drunken guests are not a good combination. During many winter weddings I photographed, guests were arranged in two lines late into the evening reception, and their sparklers were all lit at the same time (or as closely timed as it is possible to light 100 sparklers). The happy couple would then walk down between their guests with rows of sparklers either side. This served no real purpose other than it looked quite pretty and was usually a good photo opportunity. On one occasion, a drunken female guest stumbled forwards into me. I caught a strong whiff of burning and started patting my t-shirt, fearing I was on fire. I then felt a searing pain in my right cheek and realised the smell of burning was my own flesh as this drunken guest had branded me in the face with her sparkler. I had a large scab on my face for several weeks afterwards as a memento of that wedding.

We get the signal that the room is set up and the band are ready to begin their set. Jen and Matt will cut their cake and then go straight into the first dance. Rob, the usher with the loud voice, is on standby to call everyone through.

'Jen, are you going to throw your bouquet?' asks the venue's wedding coordinator.

'I don't know, I hadn't thought about it. What do you think, Matt?'

'You might as well,' says Matt. 'It's traditional.'

Despite the tackiness and slightly uncomfortable undertones, the bouquet toss is still a popular part of a wedding, even when boiled down to the bare fact that it's a bunch of drunk single women, desperate for some sign of good fortune that their moment of matrimony is just around the corner. It is quite an entertaining spectacle and always provides a great photo opportunity.

Nowadays, with such extortionate amounts of money spent on flowers – especially the bridal bouquet – the bride is often reluctant to want to part with her bouquet. The onus then falls on a willing bridesmaid to offer to sacrifice hers for the greater good. Jen's sister, Cassie, doesn't need much persuading and tells Jen she can throw hers. The idea of keeping your flowers might seem appealing, but they will soon become a sad, tired and wilted mess, you won't have the time or inclination to dry them properly, and they will be in the compost bin within a week. Or if you manage to dry them properly, they will sit on a shelf and gradually crumble away into nothing. Save yourself the hassle and offer yours up for the toss. Make the bouquet someone else's problem instead. It's just a bunch of flowers. Enjoy them. Get the photographer to take a photo of them while they look good. Then be done with them.

If you think that the bouquet toss in its current form is tacky and degrading, wait until you hear about its origins. During the middle ages, it became a symbol of good luck to claim a piece of the bride's wedding dress. This was not a symbolic act carried out in an orderly fashion. During the wedding – often soon after the ceremony – guests would all physically try to rip pieces of fabric from the bride's dress while she was wearing it. Those that succeeded in getting a piece of fabric were blessed with future happiness, whereas the bride was blessed with a shredded dress on her wedding day.

Over time, brides understandably began to object to having their dress torn apart, so the bouquet toss became a way of distracting these rabid guests from attacking her. While guests were fighting over the bouquet, the bride and groom would quickly disappear up to their bedroom to consummate the marriage. As mentioned at the beginning of this book, the consummation of marriages was often witnessed by friends and family during the bedding ceremony. After this became less commonplace, and couples decided to do the deed behind closed doors (the party-poopers), the groom would throw the bride's garter from the bedroom door as a way of evidencing that it was business time. The male guest who was first to grab the bride's garter was blessed with fertility, and presumably public opinion of being a bit pervy. The garter toss still takes place occasionally at weddings, but is far less common than it once was.

I'm a big fan of the bouquet toss. It's a harmless bit of fun and is almost always entertaining. What used to amuse me most about the bouquet toss was just how difficult some brides made it look. Having witnessed countless bouquet tosses before, and therefore considered some sort of bouquet tossing expert, brides would often ask me for advice just before the event.

'It's pretty simple,' I would say. 'You stand with your back towards the big group of women who have assembled on the dancefloor, and then you just throw your bouquet over your shoulder.'

'Got it!' they would say, only to then launch the bouquet at rocket speed into the large empty space at the far end of the room, unleashing a stampede of horny women to clamber over each other to reach the prize.

I have one sequence of wedding photos where the bride's bouquet sailed through the air, way over the heads of all of those assembled, then way over the heads of all the seated guests at the back of the room, before it crashed straight into the wall. On impact, the bouquet came apart and spread out over a five-metre blast zone. This didn't stop the women who had followed its trajectory, almost matching its speed, clawing at each other and climbing over the seated guests before grabbing a part of the bouquet. Almost all of the women got a flower, and all believed they had caught the bouquet. Everyone was happy.

I've seen bouquets that have got stuck on beams, bouquets that have hit people square in the face, bouquets that have landed on the cake, almost toppling it over, and many, many bouquets that haven't even reached as far as the front of the group.

One particularly energetic bride sent her bouquet flying into the candelabra that was strung up high in the rafters. Hot wax was sprayed over the entire room, including all of the single ladies gathered below. There were collective screams as everyone started clutching their faces and scarpered from the dancefloor as the bouquet tumbled into the middle of the empty room. Fortunately, the height of the candelabra meant that the wax had cooled slightly by the time it plastered the faces of the guests, so nobody suffered serious burns. After everyone had a quick wipe down, the bride had a successful second attempt.

Jen doesn't need advice from me. After everyone has made their way into the main barn, a group of about 20 women assemble on the dancefloor, ranging in age from six to 90. Jen stands at the front of the room, turns her back and tosses the bouquet up and over her shoulder. It sails high into the air, there's a collective scream and cheer from everyone in the room, and it falls into a mass of outstretched arms. There's a brief tangle as bodies fall on top of each other – thankfully both the six-year-old and 90-year-old were out of the action – and then the ladies part to reveal Sally, James the best man's girlfriend, clutching the bouquet. She's laughing hysterically and all eyes turn to James, who stands coyly by the door. He shakes his head, but a subtle smile suggests that it was an appropriate catch. He and Sally probably will be next.

The time has almost come for the first dance. My last first dance. But firstly, before my last first dance, Jen and Matt have the important task of cutting the cake. The cutting of the cake is one of the stalwart moments of the wedding day. It's the photo opportunity that gets all guests scrambling for their phones or cameras. It's a pivotal moment that must be witnessed by everyone. No wedding photographer would dare leave a wedding without this image. Even when I worked for Sugar Sweet Precious Memories, one of my 108 shots was the cutting of the cake. Sugar Sweet Precious Memories' photography coverage didn't extend into the evening, so I would have to get the couple to do a mock cake cutting earlier in the day, which was every bit as tedious as it sounds. But it was the cutting of the cake! I couldn't miss such a momentous occasion.

But why is this tradition so important? Spoiler alert… it isn't! It's a fucking cake that two people are sticking a knife into. Who cares? Everyone, it seems. Except, nobody actually does care. Everyone knows they are supposed to get excited about the cutting of the cake, but nobody knows why, and nobody ever looks through their photos and gets excited about seeing the cutting of the cake photo ever again. People just know that it's supposed to be important. Because it's the cutting of the cake.

In ancient Rome, small wheat cakes were baked to be eaten during wedding ceremonies. The groom would eat a piece of one loaf and then break the rest of the loaf over the bride's head. This was supposedly a symbol of good fortune. The guests would then scramble on the floor for the crumbs, hoping some of this blessing would be passed on to them. It seems like guests at weddings in the olden days spent most of the time crawling on the floor picking up scraps – crumbs, garters, bouquets, or bits of wedding dresses – and hoping for good luck.

Over time, these wheat cakes grew in size and opulence, and breaking them over the head of the bride became less practical, although it would have been quite a spectacle. And so, the tradition unfortunately faded away. I love the idea of brides and grooms hitting each other over the heads with loaves of bread – baguettes would be ideal – while guests fight it out on the floor for the crumbs. There's another ancient tradition that needs to make a comeback.

Instead, a wedding tradition emerged where small cakes were piled higher and higher – the higher the cakes were piled, the higher status and wealth this demonstrated. A new custom was born where the bride and groom were supposed to try and kiss each other over the top of the tower of cakes, without disturbing them. If they successfully kissed, happiness was guaranteed.

Presumably this game of cake Jenga became too difficult, so people began stacking larger cakes on top of each other in the sturdier recognised fashion that is seen at weddings today. It wasn't until Victorian times that white became the colour associated with wedding cakes.

The cutting of the cake is now supposed to symbolise the first job that a husband and wife do together as a couple. That's if you discount the other jobs they have already done together as a married couple, such as taking their vows together, kissing together, getting in the car together, standing together for photos, sitting together during the meal and chatting to guests together. It is, I concede, likely to be the first cake they will have cut together as a married couple. It will also be the last. Because people don't cut fucking cakes together in real life.

In true 'traditional' style, the couple should remove a slice and feed it to each other, symbolising how they will provide for each other. Most couples forgo this bit nowadays and just pose for photos with their knife meaninglessly protruding from the cake. Those that do enact the full feeding ritual often end up squashing cake in each other's face. I'm not sure what that's supposed to symbolise.

Another tradition states that the top tier of the wedding cake should be saved and enjoyed on the day of the christening of the couple's first child. Rachel's mum said she was going to put our top tier in her freezer for just that occasion. She had made the cake herself – a beautifully decorated and delicious tasting three-tier fruit cake. We told her we had no immediate plans to have children, and subtly said that if we did, it would be unlikely they would be christened. She decided to keep it 'just in case'. Layla, our first daughter, was born three years after we got married. The christening cake was mentioned again by Rachel's mum, and we politely said we would not be getting her christened. She said she would keep it 'just in case'. During the following years, the cake came up in conversation occasionally.

'You should just eat it,' I said. 'We won't be getting Layla christened.' But she held onto it 'just in case' we would change our mind.

I did consider having Layla christened, just to be done with the cake, but thought that might be a step too far. Eventually, when Layla reached the age of eight, Rachel's mum defrosted the cake from the freezer and discovered it tasted old and musty. She ate it anyway.

Jen and Matt get their cake cutting over and done with in record time. They seem to think it's as pointless as I do. It's now time for the first dance. But before it begins, I say my goodbyes to Jen and Matt. In my early days of photographing weddings, I made the mistake of trying to say goodbye when I was actually leaving, about half an hour after the first dance. By this point, the bride and groom would be busy dancing or chatting to guests and it would be a long time before I was able to get a chance to speak to them. At which point they would suddenly remember they wanted a quick photo with all of the marketing department from work. It would be 15 minutes before they were all rounded up, and then the groom decides he wants a photo of his work friends too. Next thing I know, another hour has passed, and I am still at the bloody wedding.

I soon learned a tactic to avoid this. I would say goodbye to the bride and groom before the first dance. I would tell them I was going to be there for another half an hour, but that I didn't want to disturb them on the dancefloor later. They interpreted this as me being exceptionally polite and considerate. Little did they know that it was my get-out-clause to be able to escape from their wedding at the earliest opportunity.

While we are on the subject of goodbyes, if you are getting married, don't feel obliged to say goodbye to everyone before you leave. In fact, don't feel obliged to say goodbye to anyone. There's a temptation when you have spent months and months organising the biggest day of your life to stay until the bitter end, savouring every last moment of your wedding. Don't. Leave on a high and allow the evening to end without you.

My sister and brother-in-law had the most memorable wedding exit that I have ever seen. Mid song, with the dancefloor packed with revellers, they stood on the raised stage and then jumped onto the crowd below, where they crowd-surfed on the hands of their guests. After crowd-surfing a couple of laps of the dancefloor, they were carried along the hands towards the marquee's exit and then out of the open door, through which they never returned.

If you don't fancy crowd-surfing, then either make a sneaky unannounced getaway, or get your best man, ushers and bridesmaids to gather an impromptu guard of honour, run the gauntlet of all your friends and family, and head off together to become one flesh.

I'm reluctant to leave Jen and Matt's wedding in half an hour. Soon I will be taking my last ever photograph as a professional photographer. I am not having second thoughts about my decision to retire from this industry; I feel surer than I've ever felt that I am making the right decision, but it does still feel emotional.

'Thanks again for everything, George,' says Jen, giving me a big hug.

'It has been a fantastic wedding to be a part of,' I say, 'and an absolute pleasure to photograph.'

'Yeah, thanks mate,' says Matt. 'You've been really good. I hope you have a safe journey back to Devon.'

'I would say I will recommend you to all of our friends,' says Jen, 'but I'm assuming you won't be making a habit of driving back to Northampton regularly?'

'No. Actually, I'm stopping photography completely.'

'Really? When?'

'Er… in about half an hour. This is actually my last ever wedding.'

I thought it only fair to tell them the truth.

'Shit!' says Jen. 'We weren't that difficult, were we? Have we put you off weddings completely?'

'Ha, no. I could not have asked for a nicer couple to be my final bride and groom. I honestly mean that.'

'Why are you stopping?'

'Several reasons really. It seems like the right time and I'm concentrating on writing books instead now.'

'Cool, like proper books?' says Matt.

'It depends on your definition of a proper book. Sort of, I suppose. They are non-fiction, but with a bit of a story too.'

'Will you be writing a *Confessions of a Wedding Photographer* book like my dad mentioned this morning?' says Jen.

'You never know. Maybe one day.'

'That's awesome,' she says. 'Well good luck with it and I look forward to reading one of your books.'

'Thanks. Have an amazing honeymoon and your photos will all be waiting for you when you get home. Now go and enjoy your first dance together.'

'You're going to love our choice of song,' says Jen over her shoulder, as they walk hand in hand towards the dancefloor.

'I'm intrigued,' I say. They both smile back at me as they take their place on the dancefloor. The band are all set up, but they are not holding their instruments. This song is going to be played in its original form.

EIGHTEEN

A band or DJ can make or break a wedding. If you have a lively bunch of friends and family, they will happily strut their stuff on the dancefloor to just about any form of music. Even the ringtone on someone's phone would be adequate to get some guests going. Other people take a bit more persuading to lose their inhibitions and get on that dancefloor. This is where a good band or DJ comes into its own.

Rachel and I took a gamble with our wedding band. We found them in the Yellow Pages. I'm not sure why we didn't look online, but we decided to keep it old school. They sent us a demo CD, which we really liked, and we decided to book them without bothering to go and see them play live.

During the wedding breakfast, four large middle-aged men entered the marquee, dressed in Hawaiian shirts and each carrying an inflatable guitar.

'Who are they?' asked Damo, one of my two best men.

'Er…' I gulped. 'I think they are our wedding band.'

'They look… um… they look… fun?' said Mark, my other best man.

'Wilby, at your service,' said one of the men, approaching Rachel at the top table. 'You must be Rachel.'

'I am,' said Rachel.

'And which one of you is George?'

I raised my hand like I was back at school. The fact that I was sitting next to Rachel should have been a clue, but perhaps not.

We shook hands and were introduced to the other band members, and we pointed out the stage area where they could go and set up. Then they hung around and chatted to us as we ate our meal for another 20 minutes. That's far longer than we spoke to most of our family and friends during our wedding.

Fortunately, Wilby were fantastic. The lead singer was full of energy and enthusiasm. So much so that he had to change his shirt three times during the course of their set because he sweated so profusely.

The first dance is surprisingly the cause of a lot of anxiety with some couples. Saying your vows and getting married in front of a large group of people is one thing, but the idea of dancing in front of them can bring on a whole new level of fear. This worry is all completely unnecessary. Nobody in the room is going to be assessing your dancing skills (unless you are actively trying to display some skills, which I will come to later). Those that are watching you will only see two people madly in love, enjoying the start of their married life together. I say 'those that are watching' because many of your friends and family won't be in the least bit interested about your first dance. To them it is either an annoying interruption to their evening, or just a brief interlude before the main disco kicks off.

Most of the worry stems from the fear of making a fool out of yourself on the dancefloor. This is not physically possible unless you go out of your way to make a fool out of yourself. If you want the first dance to pass without incident, all you need to do is embrace your partner and shuffle around for about a minute, before beckoning the rest of your guests to come and join you and put you out of your misery. That's really all there is to it.

There has been a trend in the last few years to liven up the first dance. Couples sometimes go to a lot of trouble to make their first dance into something more than a random shuffle around the dancefloor. If done properly, this can provide great entertainment for the guests and become a memorable part of the day. If done badly, however, it can be far more embarrassing than any awkward shuffle.

I photographed one wedding, where the groom – a tall, lanky, and slightly gawkish man – was petrified by the prospect of the first dance, perhaps more than anything else in his life. To try and allay these fears, the bride and groom enrolled on a six-month ballroom dancing class. They rehearsed an entire routine to a piece of music which they performed in front of the guests at their wedding.

Part of me found it endearing to watch. The fact that they had put so much time and effort into getting the first dance right was charming. But I also found it a little tragic. Despite the lessons and the choreography, the groom looked more uncomfortable than ever, and he would have been far less clumsy-looking had he hugged his new wife and shuffled around for a minute or two.

To the other extreme, I have photographed weddings where the bride and groom (and sometimes the entire bridal party) have choreographed a special group routine in lieu of a traditional first dance. The kind of thing that goes viral on YouTube. When done well, they can be very clever and very funny.

During the wedding of my good friend Liam, he and his wife Emma performed my favourite first dance of all time. They had practiced a routine for Chuck Berry's *Never Can Tell*. Well, I say practiced, I think they spent about 10 minutes in their kitchen discussing vaguely what they would do. What they did was flail their arms and legs around wildly for three minutes. It was full of energy, it was fun, it was chaotic, it was brilliant.

The tradition of the first dance stems back to the days of costume balls amongst the aristocracy. It was custom for the guest of honour – often the host of the party – to be the first on the dancefloor. With their partner, of course, rather than a bizarre solo dance off. This convention soon became customary during weddings too. Although, in Emily Post's popular 1922 book *Etiquette in Society, in Business, in Politics, and at Home,* she seems to advise against having a first dance, and letting the rest of the guests dance first: *'on leaving their table, the bridal party join the dancing which by now has begun in the drawing-room.'*

But that was almost 100 years ago. Some couples are so self-conscious about the first dance that they decide against having one altogether. I would suggest this is a very bad idea. The first dance is a bit naff and clichéd, but then so are weddings, and it is part of the wedding day so ingrained in tradition that it's blatantly obvious if you deliberately miss it out. I am all for going against norms, but by missing out on a first dance, you end up with lots of guests standing around the dancefloor, reluctant to step foot in the sacred square before the bride and groom have had their first dance. Doing a first dance of some sort – even if it is a ten second shuffle – at least signifies an end to the day's formalities and the start of the evening celebrations. Just get on with it.

Choosing a song for your first dance can be a real dilemma. Rachel and I didn't have a special song that we considered 'our song'. We had several songs that we mutually loved, but they were all about death or separation or loneliness. None of which were the best theme to accompany a first dance.

We picked *In My Life* by The Beatles. It wasn't a song that was particularly close to either of our hearts, but it was a song we both liked, it was timeless, and it was a love song without being too soppy.

We told our band's lead singer over the phone that we had chosen it for our first dance.

'Excellent. We know that one,' he said.

'Ah, thanks. I think we'll just play The Beatles' version from a CD,' said Rachel.

'No, it's fine. We know how to play it. It's much better coming from a live band.'

'I'm sure it is, but we like the original version thanks. We'll bring a CD along.'

'No need. We will do The Beatles proud. Trust us.'

'But…'

It didn't matter how strongly Rachel pleaded, Wilby's lead singer was adamant that they were going to play it, and we assumed that this level of confidence would mean that perhaps his version was in fact better than The Beatles.

It wasn't. But it was certainly memorable.

When he had said that they knew how to play it, he meant that HE knew how to play it. The rest of the band didn't even pick up their instruments to play along. Instead, we had Wilby's lead singer – a large sweaty man in a Hawaiian shirt – standing at a keyboard under a giant spotlight in the middle of the stage. He sang it vaguely in tune and seemed to be playing most of the correct notes, but there was something about his voice and the way he was bashing the shit out of the keyboard, that made it particularly comical. There was no chance of either Rachel or me feeling self-conscious during our first dance, as we were too busy laughing at the wedding singer. After about a minute of the song, we beckoned the other guests to come and join us, and from then on, Wilby excelled themselves.

I never asked couples what their first dance was going to be. As a photographer, it was my job to know the running order of the day intimately and be familiar with all the timings and details in advance so that I could be ready and prepared. I would ask couples what the expected time of their first dance was, but I liked to keep that one element of surprise when they embraced on the empty dancefloor surrounded by their friends and family. Nine times out of ten I would be familiar with their song. Occasionally their choice would be an obscure song I had not heard before, but had some personal connection to the couple, and it almost always seemed like an appropriate choice.

So, when I was photographing Hannah and Ian's wedding in the function room of a local golf club, I smiled as the familiar piano introduction of one of Adele's most popular songs filled the room. I looked around and all the guests smiled too, their cameras all poised, gazing in the direction of the happy couple. Something wasn't right, though. The happy couple were looking rather unhappy.

'I heard… that you're… settled down,' sang Adele. *'…that you… found a girl… and you're… married now'.*

Aww, such a beautiful song. Great choice! But why didn't the couple look happy? They were still shuffling half-heartedly around the dancefloor but mouthing something to each other and looking anxiously at the DJ, who just smiled back at them.

'I heard… that your… dreams came true… I guess she gave you things I didn't give to you.'

Wait a minute! This doesn't sound very romantic. I mean, it's an incredible song, but a bit of an odd choice for a first dance. Those around the room could sense that something was not right from how agitated Hannah and Ian looked. Ian had now broken away from Hannah and was striding purposefully over to the DJ and was trying to shout something to him over the music.

It was clearly the wrong song. The DJ cupped his hand to his ear trying to make out what Ian was saying. But then Adele started wailing again, *'sometimes it lasts in love, but sometimes it HUUUUURTS INNNSTEEEAD.'*

Alright Adele! Shut the fuck up! Enough already. We get the message. This is supposed to be a happy occasion.

The DJ eventually cut the song and began frantically flicking through his box of CDs looking for the correct track.

Ian walked over to me.

'He got the wrong Adele song. He's supposed to be playing *Make You Feel My Love*. The one he played is a bloody breakup song, isn't it? Probably not the best thing to be played for a first dance.'

The DJ was looking more and more agitated. He was now scrolling frantically through his phone and shaking his head. Ian walked back over to him. Lots more head-shaking followed. Ian returned and told the best man and me that the DJ didn't have *Make You Feel My Love*.

'He doesn't have it. There's no mobile signal or Wi-Fi here so he can't get it online either.'

The best man started scrolling through his phone to see if he had it. I felt a bit useless standing there, so I had a look at my phone too. While everyone else in the developed world now owned a smartphone, I still had a Nokia 3210. I still stared at it hopefully, trying to look useful.

'Any luck?' asked the groom.

'Sorry,' said the best man. 'I think I used to have it.'

'I've only got *Snake*, I'm afraid,' I added, holding up my retro piece of crap.

Ian managed a smile for the first time in a while.

We started subtly asking around if any of the guests had the song. There was a lot of headshaking and then the husband of one of the bridesmaids remembered he might have it on an old iPod in his car's glovebox. He dashed from the room while Ian and Hannah loitered awkwardly on the dancefloor. The mortified DJ continued to flick through his box of CDs for the 400th time, as though it would miraculously appear. Eventually, the bridesmaid's husband returned clutching an iPod high above his head like it was the World Cup.

The DJ was able to hook it up to his sound desk and Adele's dulcet tones, this time singing the correct song, filled the room, much to the relief of Hannah, Ian and the mortified DJ.

NINETEEN

The opening chords to Jen and Matt's first dance sound out through the PA system and I'm instantly choked up. The song they have chosen is *First Day of My Life* by Bright Eyes. The reason it has made me emotional, and the reason Jen said she knew I would like it, is that I used it as the backing track for the slideshow of photos that I showed to Jen and Matt at our first meeting.

It is not a particularly famous song, and very few couples had ever heard it when I showed them my photos, but many would comment on the song and several asked me who it was by and what album it was on (it is from the album *I'm Wide Awake, It's Morning* – one of my top five albums of all time). I think this is the third or perhaps fourth time a bride and groom have chosen it as their first dance after hearing it for the first time with my wedding portfolio.

It's a wonderful choice of song. Rachel and I would have had it for our first dance, only it wasn't released until two years after we married. It's a love song, but not overly gushy and with a more realistic outlook of love and relationships. It says how relationships can be difficult and you will have to work at them.

Because you do. Marriage isn't always easy and couples don't always live happily ever after. According to recent statistics, a staggering 42% of marriages in the UK end in divorce. This is the seventh highest in the world, behind Germany, USA, Russia, France, Spain and Luxembourg with a whopping 87% divorce rate. If you are a wedding photographer in Luxembourg, don't waste too much time putting together your wedding albums.

I know of several couples who have split up since I photographed their weddings. Given the statistics, it was inevitable. In some of these cases it was obvious from my time with them that their marriage wasn't going to last. There was no spark. No chemistry. No love. And, in the incident with the little shit Dean, no juice. There were other couples that I was surprised about when I heard of their split, and then looking back there were clues that perhaps they weren't as suited as I thought. Very occasionally, I confess, I almost hoped that a couple would split up, because either the bride or groom was a total arse and I didn't think they deserved their lovely other half. And there were some couples that on the surface looked perfect for each other – and perhaps at the time they were – but then in the years following the wedding, cracks began to show, and before long they were separated. People and circumstances change and it's natural that some couples will drift apart. I don't think any of this should undermine weddings, or marriage for that matter, and we should never take for granted the importance of companionship.

I photographed the memorable wedding of Rob and Jess, one of the loveliest couples I ever had the pleasure of photographing. I met them at their flat for a few pre-wedding meetings, and they were great company and easy to talk to. Rob was just getting into photography and was full of admiration that I was a professional. He spoke to me more about photography than he did about his wedding plans, and I had an email from him after our first meeting saying he planned to enrol on a photography course after my suggestion.

Rob and Jess's wedding day was unbelievably wet – one of the wettest I ever photographed – but they were smiley throughout, and full of love for each other. During the wedding speeches, I learned from the best man that Rob had been rushed to hospital at the age of 16 and diagnosed with a rare heart condition. He was transferred to a specialist unit, during which time his heart stopped several times, and he underwent an emergency heart transplant. I chatted to Rob all about it during the evening reception and was in awe of everything he had been through and the extraordinary recovery he had made.

A little over a year after their wedding, I received an email from Jess. She told me that Rob had suffered a heart attack while they were on holiday in Rome together and had sadly died. He was 28.

Jess told me Rob had been inspired by our chats about photography and had continued to pursue it passionately as a hobby. I went to Rob's funeral the following week. All those attending were asked to wear bright colours, and every inch of the large crematorium was full. I had arrived early but still only managed to squeeze into a standing space in the aisle. Jess read a beautiful and incredibly emotional eulogy, somehow managing to stay composed throughout, as everybody else in the room wept. It was a stark reminder of how fragile life is and why we should hold the ones we love that little bit tighter.

Halfway through the first dance, Jen and Matt beckon their friends and family to join them on the dancefloor. It's a slow acoustic song, so this isn't a cue for people to start body-popping across the room. Instead, couples take each other by the hand and head out onto the dancefloor. Matt's parents – now separated – give each other a quick hug before joining their respective partners and dancing alongside Jen and Matt. James, the best man and his girlfriend Sally – who is still firmly clasping the bouquet she caught – look very much like this is a rehearsal for their own first dance. One of Matt's ushers tentatively asks one of the bridesmaids for a dance. She smiles coyly then takes his hand. Jen's mum and dad look as happy as a newly married couple – despite whatever mischief Jen's mum got up to on the hen do in Benidorm. Matt's grandparents, both in their late 80s, take to the floor and begin an ambitious rendition of *The Waltz* that requires dodging around all the other couples on the dancefloor.

It's a beautiful scene to watch, and an illustration of what a wonderful thing love is. I work my way around the outside of the dancefloor, trying to capture this moment in my photos. After only a minute, the song comes to an end, there's a brief pause of a couple of seconds, and then the band launch into a high-tempo version of Bryan Adams' *Summer of '69*. The couples all take a step back from their partners and swap their loving embrace for an air guitar each. It's party time! Those lurking around the edge of the room reluctant to join in for the slow dance now swarm the dancefloor, and I search for safety at higher ground. I make my way to some steps at the edge of the room from where I can get a good vantage point of the dancefloor without getting trampled.

I spend the next half an hour snapping away, getting photographs of as many different people dancing as possible. After half an hour, there is usually a lull as the dancefloor empties slightly, as people take a breather, refill their drinks, go to the toilet, or join the queue for the evening buffet. This signifies my time to leave. My work here is done.

When I set out to write this book, I expected it to be a series of stories and anecdotes mocking the whole idea of weddings, tales of bridezillas and people losing their shit over the colour scheme. But it didn't turn out like that. Yes, I encountered some bridezilla moments, but given the hysteria of the entire industry, it's no wonder brides and grooms become so consumed in their own wedding that they forget the whole point of their marriage. Choosing to spend the rest of your life with someone. Now that's what is important. Not all the glittery bullshit that surrounds your wedding, but the decision itself to get married and then everything that follows.

Once you have decided to spend the rest of your life with someone, the details of your wedding don't matter. Not the dress, not the readings, not the venue, not the first dance, not the flowers, not the favours, and not the colour scheme. Get married however you like. Stick to traditions, if they take your fancy. Ignore others, if you consider them outdated. Or be a trailblazer and create your own traditions. Do it your way. Don't listen to the advice of anyone else (especially not a cynical former wedding photographer like me) and, providing you love your partner, however you decide to get married, it will be the best day of your life.

Despite my cynicism, I realised while writing this book how much I love weddings. I always have. So much about them is bollocks, but then most traditions are. It's the familiarity and the predictability of these traditions that help create the magic.

I'm going to miss photographing weddings. I will miss the palpable feeling of nervousness and anticipation during the bridal preparations in the morning. I'll miss that unmistakable church wedding smell. I'll miss seeing the groom have the sudden panicked realisation that today is the day, and then the look on his face when he turns to see his bride for the first time. I'll miss the butterflies I feel at the sounding of the church organ. I might, I confess, even miss hearing *A Lovely Love Story* by Edward Monkton. I'll miss that look of pure happiness as the bride and groom take their first steps down the aisle as a married couple. I'll miss the mischievous faces on the guests as they prepare to throw their confetti. I'll miss that feeling of satisfaction when I have worked my way through all the formal group shots and ticked the last one off my list, and discovering that I did have a memory card in my camera for the duration. I'll miss pointless favours. I'll miss my free meals. I'll miss listening to different wedding speeches every weekend; each one very different, but very much the same as the one before. I'll miss calamitous bouquet tosses. I'll miss seeing how excited people get about two people sticking a knife into a fucking cake. I'll miss the anticipation of hearing what song the bride and groom have chosen for their first dance, and then watching two people madly in love shuffle awkwardly on the dancefloor. But mostly, I'll miss the sense of realisation I felt at every wedding I ever worked at, of what a huge privilege it was to be trusted with photographing the most important day of these couples' lives.

I take one last look at the venue from outside as I return to my car. A chorus of voices from inside sing along to the band's rendition of *Hi Ho Silver Lining*. The bridal magazine is still on the passenger seat where I left it. I've finished reading it and I don't think I will have any need to look at it again, so I tuck it under the windscreen wipers of James the best man's car. Then I climb into my car, turn the key in the ignition and begin my long drive home, no longer a professional photographer, leaving this whole wedding circus behind and excited about what lies ahead.

If you enjoyed reading *How Not to Get Married*, I would be extremely grateful if you would consider posting a short review on Amazon. Reviews are hugely important for authors, so any way in which you can help spread the word is greatly appreciated. Thank you.

I have written SIX other books. All are available on Amazon and details can be found on the following pages.

Please check out my Facebook page where you can view the photos that accompany my other books and keep up-to-date with what I am working on.

www.facebook.com/georgemahood

I have a useless website that I don't update at all, but there is a mailing list signup page if you would like to be one of the first to hear of my new books. Signed paperback copies of all my books are available from my website's 'shop'.

www.georgemahood.com

I am on Twitter for general ramblings: **@georgemahood**
And Instagram too **@georgemahood**

Or you can drop me an email with any comments, feedback or criticism. It's always great to hear from readers.

george@georgemahood.com

If you, or someone you know, has gone through a difficult breakup, I would highly recommend **Break Up and Shine** by my good friend Marissa Walter.

In *Break Up and Shine*, counsellor and author Marissa Walter shares powerful lessons learned from her divorce to guide you through your emotional pain and see it as an opportunity to move on to a happier life.

Break Up and Shine combines personal experience with inspired wisdom and practical advice, to support you in moving on and making life after the end of your relationship your happiest time yet.

Break Up and Shine is available on Amazon

ACKNOWLEDGEMENTS

Firstly, thanks to you for reading my ramblings. This book has been a bit of a departure from my usual stuff, but it was a fun book to write and I hope you enjoyed it too.

This book would not have been possible if I had not been trusted by all those brides and grooms to photograph their special day. Thank you! If you are one of the brides or grooms that I photographed, then your wedding was definitely my favourite.

Thank you to all the other wedding suppliers I got to know during my decade in the industry – florists, caterers, musicians, videographers, coordinators. Having others to laugh and share stories with made my job so much more enjoyable.

Thanks to Miriam for her valuable comments after reading an early draft. Big thanks to Becky Beer – my pilkunnussija-in-chief – for being such an eagle-eyed proofreader. Please check out her *Bookaholic Bex* blog and Facebook page. Thanks to Robin Hommel for her additional proofreading help.

To research some of the history of weddings, I turned to other books and articles about the subject. The following books provided me with help and inspiration – *One Perfect Day: The Selling of the American Wedding* by Rebecca Mead, *Committed: A Love Story* by Elizabeth Gilbert, *Confessions of a Wedding Planner* by Tamryn Kirby. Thank you also to the countless and nameless historians and scholars whose research into weddings has now spread far and wide over the internet. Thanks also, of course, to Wikipedia.

Lastly, thank you to Rachel, not only being my editor and providing such valuable feedback and support, but for choosing to spend the rest of her life with me.

OTHER BOOKS BY GEORGE MAHOOD

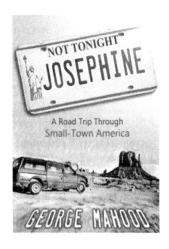

NOT TONIGHT, JOSEPHINE:
A Road Trip Through Small-Town America

Two Brits, George and Mark, set off from New York City to explore the back roads of America. In this calamity-ridden travel tale, George sets out in true clichéd fashion to discover the real America.

Throw in plenty of run-ins with the police, rapidly dwindling finances and Josephine – the worst car in the world – and you have all the ingredients for a classic American road trip. Will George and Mark make it all the way to California?

And then there is Rachel, George's girlfriend, left back in England. Would travelling to the United States without her turn out to be the stupidest decision he had ever made?

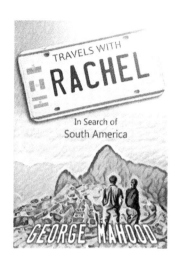

TRAVELS WITH RACHEL:
In Search of South America

Knee-deep in a swamp in the depths of the Bolivian jungle, hunting for anacondas in a pair of sandals, it occurred to George that perhaps he should have booked that all-inclusive honeymoon to the Maldives after all.

Join George and Rachel on their hilarious journey through the wilds of Ecuador, Peru and Bolivia, as they climb volcanoes, fish for piranhas, trek through the Amazon rainforest, take death-defying bus rides, sample some of the continent's strangest delicacies, and try to get to Machu Picchu.

Armed only with a basic knowledge of Spanish, small backpacks, and bags of enthusiasm, they set off together on what promised to be a life-changing adventure.

FREE COUNTRY:
A Penniless Adventure the Length of Britain

The plan is simple. George and Ben have three weeks to cycle 1000 miles from the bottom of England to the top of Scotland. There is just one small problem... they have no bikes, no clothes, no food and no money. Setting off in just a pair of Union Jack boxer shorts, they attempt to rely on the generosity of the British public for everything from food to accommodation, clothes to shoes, and bikes to beer.

During the most hilarious adventure, George and Ben encounter some of Great Britain's most eccentric and extraordinary characters and find themselves in the most ridiculous situations. Free Country is guaranteed to make you laugh (you may even shed a tear). It will restore your faith in humanity and leave you with a big smile on your face and a warm feeling inside.

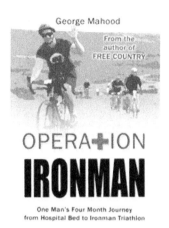

George Mahood

From the author of FREE COUNTRY

OPERA+ION
IRONMAN

One Man's Four Month Journey
from Hospital Bed to Ironman Triathlon

OPERATION IRONMAN:
One Man's Four Month Journey from Hospital Bed to Ironman Triathlon

Operation Ironman follows George Mahood's inspiring and entertaining journey from a hospital bed to an Ironman triathlon. After major surgery to remove a spinal cord tumour, George set himself the ultimate challenge:

a 2.4 mile swim,

a 112 mile bike ride,

and a 26.2 mile run,

all to be completed within 16 hours.

He couldn't swim more than a length of front crawl, he had never ridden a proper road bike, he had not run further than 10k in 18 months... and he had never worn Lycra.

He had four months to prepare.

Could he do it?

EVERY DAY IS A HOLIDAY

George Mahood had a nice, easy, comfortable life. But something was missing. He was stuck in a routine of working, changing nappies and cleaning up cat sick. He felt like he was missing out on a lot of what the world had to offer.

He then discovered that it was Bubble Wrap Appreciation Day. The day after that was National Curmudgeon Day, and the day after that was Inane Answering Machine Message Day. He realised that somebody somewhere had created these holidays, believing that they were important enough to warrant their own official day. Surely he should therefore be more appreciative of their existence? So he decided to try and celebrate them all. He hoped that at the end of the challenge he would be transformed into a happier, more intelligent and more content person.

Follow George on his hilarious, life changing adventure as he tries to balance his normal life with a wealth of new experiences, people, facts and ridiculous situations. It's a rip-roaring, life-affirming, roller-coaster of a ride, where every day is a holiday.

Printed in Great Britain
by Amazon

84671328R00140